Political Terror in
Communist Systems

Political Terror in Communist Systems

Alexander Dallin and George W. Breslauer

Stanford University Press, Stanford, California 1970

Stanford University Press, Stanford, California
© *1970 by the Board of Trustees of the*
Leland Stanford Junior University
Printed in the United States of America
ISBN 0-8047-0727-8 LC 71-119502

Foreword

Sometimes it seems that most Western social scientists specializing in the study of Communist societies belong to a "They're not really crazy" school of analysis. By contrast, the average observer of Communism in power, without expert knowledge of the countries and regimes involved, might well conclude that Communist nations are ruled by tyrannical lunatics. The specialist, however, is often able to show that policies appearing at first glance to be irrational, utopian, or ill-advised are sensible—even functional—and conducive to socioeconomic progress when considered in terms of preexisting obstacles to social change or the political culture of a social system. Such analyses are particularly relevant if the system studied is one in which indigenous Communists have assumed the leadership of authentic revolutions—in the Soviet Union, Yugoslavia, and China, for example.

There are both limits and dangers to this scholarly orientation, however. The specialist runs the risk of finding a developmental rationale for every policy a regime adopts, whether or not one exists, and of ignoring both the diverse inputs into policy and the occasionally disastrous outcomes. Nowhere is this danger greater than in the analysis of political terror, as it commonly occurs in Communist mobilization systems. It may well be, for example, that terroristic purges in Communist regimes perform the function of recruiting and retiring personnel into and out of the party, a particularly difficult task to carry out routinely in such regimes for structural and ideological reasons. However, the independent observer still wants to ask,

in response to the old Leninist cliché about not being able to
make an omelette without breaking eggs, "How many eggs do
you have to break in order to make a one-egg omelette?" The
impact of terror on the authority, ideology, and morale of a
revolutionary regime is every bit as important a point of understanding as the functions terror performs. Very possibly the
most damning criticism of Communism in power is that its prac-
titioners have been unable to think of any way other than terror
to bring about the changes they desire.

   The great strength of this study is that the authors avoid the
errors of both "normative functionalism" and culture-bound
moralism. They analyze both the revolutionary goals achieved
through terror and the legacy of terror, both the omelette and
the broken eggshells. Dallin and Breslauer are thus able to make
a major contribution to the comparative analysis of Communist
systems.

   This study grew out of the Workshop on the Comparative
Study of Communism, sponsored by the Planning Committee
for Comparative Communist Studies of the American Council
of Learned Societies and held during the summer of 1968 at the
Center for Advanced Study in the Behavioral Sciences, Stanford
University.* Originally planned as one paper for a collaborative
volume on how and why Communist systems change, this study,
perhaps the most ambitious research project undertaken by any
two participants in the Workshop, grew into a book-length analysis. A modified version of chapter six of this book has been included in a larger collective effort, *Change in Communist Systems*, edited by Chalmers Johnson and published in 1970 by
Stanford University Press. For further information on the
Workshop on the Comparative Study of Communism, 1968,
readers should consult the account of the seminars themselves

---

* The Planning Committee consisted of Alexander Dallin, Chairman (Columbia Uni-
versity), R. V. Burks (Wayne State University), Alexander Eckstein (University of
Michigan), Chalmers Johnson (University of California, Berkeley), Joseph LaPalombara
(Yale University), Gordon B. Turner (American Council of Learned Societies), and
Ezra F. Vogel (Harvard University).

written by R. V. Burks and published in the *Newsletter on Comparative Studies of Communism*, II: 2 (June 1969), 2–11.

The subject considered by Dallin and Breslauer is one of the most difficult and most heartbreaking of any that the contemporary political analyst can set for himself. In a world still plagued by violence and terrorism, reason, it would seem, is no antidote. But it is the tool for beginning to find a remedy. Dallin and Breslauer here contribute the first requisite, a reasoned diagnosis of the conditions in which Communist terror is used and the functions it serves.

CHALMERS JOHNSON

April 1970

Preface

This work grew out of our curiosity about the nature and role of terror in Communist systems, as one of the papers generated by the Workshop on the Comparative Study of Communism described by Chalmers Johnson in the Foreword to this book. We soon discovered, to our surprise, that the theoretical literature on political terror was not nearly so well developed as we had expected and that, in particular, there are almost no systematic efforts in this field to compare and to explain the differences among various Communist (and non-Communist) systems. The excuse, then, for expanding our paper to the dimensions of a modest book lies primarily in the interest that we ourselves discovered in the problems here raised and in the absence of studies to which we could turn for adequate answers.

Our concern has been primarily to provide a broad framework for analysis—inevitably, it seemed to us, multidisciplinary in approach because of the very nature of the subject matter—rather than to reconstruct the actual course of developments in any, let alone all, Communist polities. We have tried to provide enough illustrative detail to make our references meaningful to those who study particular Communist countries. We have found it helpful, for our own use, to take cognizance of and at times to take issue with other writings on terror as it relates to Communism. We have referred to other works dealing with political terror and purges in general and with the experience of individuals in various periods and in countries under Communist rule. These illustrations are meant to be suggestive rather than exhaustive of the problem.

We do wish to record explicitly that our attempt here to deal with terror as a phenomenon that can be rationally analyzed in no way implies any moral indifference or callousness toward its human impact or social costs. And we recognize that any endeavor to provide a general conceptual framework cannot do justice to or account for the wide range of specific exceptions that could be explained—if our approach holds true—only by the unique circumstances of each given case.

If this volume contains a moderate amount of current social-science jargon, this is not meant either as an attempt at esoteric communication with putative colleagues, or as a stab at obfuscation. It is rather because, in a field replete with terms each of which has in common parlance a wide variety of connotations, the use of some political-science and sociological terms helps provide a minimum of definitional and conceptual rigor and clarity—or so we have hoped. We earnestly trust that this will not detract from the intelligibility of the presentation for those who have valiantly resisted exposure to such language.

This little book is truly the work of joint authorship. After a summer gratefully spent at the Center for Advanced Study in the Behavioral Sciences at Stanford, California, where an outline of this study was produced, each of us returned to his home base—one, at Columbia University; the other, at the University of Michigan. The final product, as it is presented here, is the result of numerous drafts, letters, and ideas exchanged and of conversations in the course of which each of us contributed to and revised the concepts, evidence, analysis, and formulations.

We owe an intellectual debt to several colleagues who are probably not aware of their vicarious contribution through their writings, which we have sought to acknowledge in the notes without of course inflicting any responsibility on them. These are, in particular, Amitai Etzioni, Chalmers Johnson, Paul Kecskemeti, and Barrington Moore. In addition, we are appreciative of the stimulating ideas and critiques from friends and colleagues, and especially from Zbigniew Brzezinski, Joel Glassman, and Richard Lowenthal.

Two graduate students at Columbia, Barry Liebman and Stanley Riveles, helped competently with some of the research. Mrs. Mildred O'Brien of New York City deserves special thanks for her skillful and devoted clerical assistance well above and beyond the call of duty.

If finally we must express our gratitude to Anne Firth Murray for her editorial labors, this is not meant to be a perfunctory acknowledgment: her incisive and informed comments and queries forced us to rethink many a formulation and materially helped give this volume its present shape.

GEORGE W. BRESLAUER
ALEXANDER DALLIN

March 1970

Contents

Political Terror in
Communist Systems

1 Concepts and Contexts

> The foundation of popular government in time of revolution
> is at once virtue and terror: virtue, without which terror is fatal;
> terror, without which virtue is powerless.
>
> *Robespierre*

Although political terror has been called the linchpin of totalitarianism, doubt remains about its place, its importance, and its purposes.[1] Indeed, there is a surprising paucity of discussion about its functions and dynamics in any system.

By "political terror" we mean the arbitrary use, by organs of political authority, of severe coercion against individuals or groups, the credible threat of such use, or the arbitrary extermination of such individuals or groups.[2] In this book we seek to determine the place of terror in Communist systems and to relate it to general theories of political dynamics. We also seek to identify the range of functions of political terror as well as its functional equivalents. Finally, we seek to explore variations in the use of terror among different Communist systems and the reasons for them.

[1] For interpretations stressing the centrality of terror in totalitarian systems, see, for example, Hannah Arendt, *The Origins of Totalitarianism*; Carl Friedrich and Zbigniew Brzezinski, *Totalitarian Dictatorship and Autocracy*; and Merle Fainsod's valuable analysis *How Russia Is Ruled*, ch. 13. Stimulating discussions are to be found in Barrington Moore, *Terror and Progress—USSR*; and Brzezinski, *The Permanent Purge*. See also Thomas Thornton, "Terror as a Weapon of Political Agitation." Full publication data are given in the Bibliography, pp. 147–63.

[2] Our definition is broadly consistent with the prevailing use of the term. Some of the insights in recent writings on political violence have proven useful to the present effort. See, for example, Henry Bienen, *Violence and Social Change* and the literature reviewed therein; and Sheldon Wolin, "Violence and the Western Political Tradition." Barrington Moore, whose analysis has proved to be among the most perceptive, comments in an epilogue to the paperback edition of his *Soviet Politics: The Dilemma of Power*, pp. 428–29, that in the original version (1950) he had underestimated the role of Stalinist terror. Carl Friedrich, on the other hand, now believes that he previously overestimated "the significance of [the element of terror in] the totalitarian syndrome" ("Totalitarianism: Recent Trends," p. 39).

E. V. Walter's *Terror and Resistance* appeared after this study was completed. (See also his earlier "Power and Violence.") Although Walter's conclusions tend in a different direction, his approach in many respects coincides with ours. But whereas he considers all terror to be violence designed to control (p. 14), and Alfred Meyer speaks of terror

Coercion, Control, and Compliance

Political terror as an instrument of power[3] is best seen as a form of coercion, which in turn is one major means of political control.[4] By "political control" we mean the shaping and channeling of political behavior either to secure compliance with particular directives or to mold attitudes so as to assure political stability through the voluntary acceptance of a given authority structure, its norms of social conduct, and its directives.[5]

Thus conceived, all social and political control requires a system of sanctions that consists of three exhaustive types: "normative power" (also referred to as positive or symbolic power), commonly called persuasion and including socialization, education, and the offer of prestige, recognition, or love; "material power" (also referred to as technical or utilitarian power), commonly called incentives and including such forms as wages, rewards, bonuses, bribes, and promotions; and "coercive power" (also referred to as negative or physical power), commonly called coercion, and including such forms as fines, penalties, terror, and regulatory and police power.

All social systems, which are based on a division of labor and a division of roles, require power to assure the acceptance of dominant values or the implementation of policy decisions.[6]

---

as "violence, applied or threatened" (*The Soviet Political System*, p. 318), terror in our usage does not necessarily include violence: just as some violence involves no terror, some terror (e.g., intimidation) requires no violence.

Joseph Roucek, "Sociological Elements of a Theory of Terror and Violence," p. 166, speaks of terror as "a person or thing or practice that causes intense fear or suffering, whose aim is to intimidate, subjugate, especially as a political weapon or policy." Herbert Marcuse, *Soviet Marxism*, p. 112, defines terror as the "centralized, methodical application of incalculable violence." Recognizing the inadequacy of the definition, Jerzy Gliksman ("Social Prophylaxis as a Form of Soviet Terror," p. 61) uses "to terrorize" to mean "to instill intense fear of punishment." See also the discussion in William Frame, "Dialectical Historicism and the Terror in Chinese Communism."

[3] Power may be considered, most simply, as the capacity to exert influence.

[4] For a discussion of the concepts as here used, see Franz Neumann, "Approaches to the Study of Political Power," in his *The Democratic and the Authoritarian State*; Moore, *Terror and Progress*; and especially Amitai Etzioni's *A Comparative Analysis of Complex Organizations*, pp. 3–27, and his *The Active Society*. A somewhat similar approach is used in Ezra Vogel, "Voluntarism and Social Control." For an earlier analysis adumbrating a rather similar approach, see Bertrand Russell, *Power*, ch. 3. For discussions of the changing usage of the concepts of social and political control, see Richard LaPiere, *A Theory of Social Control*; and *International Encyclopedia of the Social Sciences*, XIV, 381–402.

[5] This use of the term does not, of course, include outright physical extermination.

[6] We speak of "role" as a "complex of behavior expectations associated with a given social position or status" (Ralf Dahrendorf, *Class and Class Conflict*, p. 120). "Norms,"

Although governments do not explicitly decide what types of power to apply and in what proportions, they may be expected normally to use all three types. As Franz Neumann has pointed out, it is precisely the mix of these forms in the system of sanctions that constitutes a central problem for the political scientist as well as for the practitioner.[7]

Whereas coercion is most effective in securing short-term compliance, it is least effective in securing subjective commitment over long periods.[8] Normative power, in contrast, is the most economical and thorough but also the most difficult to manipulate with discrimination. Coercion is most effective in deterring and punishing behavior; it is least effective in promoting voluntary cooperation with commitment. Yet, as Amitai Etzioni has sought to show, modern society tends to require for its complex and multifarious role tasks the use of resources, such as goodwill, creative and critical intelligence, and independence of judgment, that cannot be harnessed by coercive means alone.

Rational policy-makers in any system may be expected to prefer to avoid the costs and penalties of widespread coercion, but to do so they must be able to draw on other forms of power—in particular, on effective socialization. Communist leaders, too, presumably look forward to a shift of emphasis from coercive to normative relations with their citizenry. Yet instead of promot-

---

then, are "role requirements, or standards of expected performance which govern roles"; and shared "values" are symbols that "establish the conscious solidarity that characterizes men joined together in a moral community" (Chalmers Johnson, *Revolutionary Change*, pp. 41–42).

[7] Coercion may of course include the withholding or withdrawing of normative or material power. That is, sanction systems contain both negative and positive dimensions. The degree of compliance and control achieved is determined in large measure by the types and proportions of positive and negative sanctions employed. In his *Class and Class Conflict in Industrial Society*, Ralf Dahrendorf argues that complex modern societies are integrated by predominantly coercive means. This leads him to posit that social control is best studied in terms of negative sanctions. (See "Homo Sociologicus," in his *Essays in the Theory of Society*, pp. 19–87.) Although we agree that negative sanctions and constraints are more ubiquitous features of modern society than are positive rewards, we believe that a study of compliance and control must account for both. Indeed, the two are opposite sides of the same coin.

[8] A reservation is required if we think of the population as consisting of internally cleft and conflicting groups. Thus, it is possible for a revolutionary elite to seek, and secure, greater support by one group (e.g., the landless peasantry) by coercive action against another (e.g., the landlords). We shall therefore distinguish between victims of coercion and target groups of the process. The victims and targets are identical where the liquidation is kept secret (in what might be called "hermetic terror"). On the other hand, "demonstration terror" (or "reverberating terror") may induce diffuse terror reactions well beyond the intended target groups. See also below, pp. 26, 35, 62–63, 119–20, 127–28.

ing socialization, coercion maximizes alienation—even when it secures compliant behavior—and thus tends to render more difficult the regime's task of achieving popular legitimacy.[9]

Not all coercion, of course, is terror. Although at times the boundaries between terror and other, "calculable," forms of coercion are vague, coercive means other than terror leave the victim an opportunity to orient himself and foresee the consequences of his action; terror typically does not. It tends to erode the relatively stable pattern of expectations required by social organization. Under conditions of terror, even conformity does not assure security or survival. As Zbigniew Brzezinski has put it, under terror "failure to adjust can mean extinction of life. But success in adjusting . . . does not guarantee either liberty or safety."[10] It is this element of arbitrariness—or, from the vantage point of the citizen, the unpredictability—in the use of terror that is its distinguishing mark.[11]

Of all the instruments in the arsenal of the state, terror is the ultimate weapon, to be applied when all else has failed, although in fact it has often been used well short of such emergency. In some respects it is to domestic policy what war is to foreign affairs: normally any government will prefer to use more limited or conventional means to secure its ends. But the very capability of a regime to resort to terror—if credible—may allow it to accomplish its purposes without the use of terror. Indeed, the threat of arbitrary coercion may be just as alienating as its use.[12]

Finally, the ambiguity of the term, terror, itself creates se-

[9] "Legitimacy" and "support" are used interchangeably in this book, unless otherwise indicated. A regime's legitimacy is defined in terms of its right to wield political authority (including the right to coerce) in a manner accepted by those sharing its system of values. (See Johnson, *Revolutionary Change*, p. 30; S. M. Lipset, *Political Man*, p. 64; Gabriel Almond and G. B. Powell, *Comparative Politics*, p. 18.)

[10] *The Permanent Purge*, p. 1.

[11] Thornton ("Terror as a Weapon of Political Agitation," pp. 81–82) correctly suggests that terror is most effective when it is indiscriminate in appearance but highly discriminate in fact.

[12] The various sanctions are essentially anticipatory, for they are intended to secure compliance or conformity because the target individual is sensitive to the punishment he may expect if he fails to comply or conform, or to the reward he may expect if he does. But the effectiveness of the sanction also depends on the relative value that the individual places on the particular set of symbols, rewards, or deprivations.

mantic difficulties; it refers to the system or policy of terror,[13] to the process of inducing terror, as well as to the condition or effect of being terrorized. Independent of the application of purposive or "transitive" terror, then, there may well exist in a society a widespread condition of terror—a pervasive atmosphere of anxiety. Even a mistaken assumption or vague rumor in the population that arbitrary repression is about to occur may be as productive of terror as its purposive use.

Terror and the Developmental Hypothesis

The major argument that follows assumes that Communist systems may be regarded as "developing" polities, which experience certain characteristic dynamics. In the period immediately following the seizure of power, especially in relatively poor and underdeveloped countries, a revolutionary regime tends to rely heavily on coercion to consolidate its power, by effectively eliminating actual and potential enemies within the territory under its control and by deterring hostile acts. Even if it comes to power with a measure of popular support, a revolutionary regime may have no meaningful alternative to the use of coercion, for it does not possess the base for adequate material incentives for the rank and file (which, moreover, may be ideologically unacceptable to Communist elites, particularly in the regime's early phases); and it cannot quickly create sufficient normative dedication to the regime or to common values, because socialization and indoctrination at best require time.

Both the purposes and the functions of political terror are many.[14] After a Communist elite seizes power, terror helps to assure survival and consolidate power; sometimes it is used along with other forms of violence such as civil war. This initial use, intended essentially to eliminate or neutralize resistance,

---

[13] Walter (*Terror and Resistance*, pp. 5–6) defines a system of terror as "a sphere of relationships controlled by the terror process."

[14] Functions are "observable objective consequences, and not subjective dispositions (aims, motives, purposes)." See Robert Merton, *Social Theory and Social Structure*, p. 78. As for the decision-makers' purposes in invoking terror, we can do little more than guess. We are here not concerned with Merton's distinction between "manifest" and "latent" functions. See also Dorothy Emmet, *Function, Purpose, and Powers*, and Ernest Nagel, *The Structure of Science*, pp. 522–25.

is inherently limited; indeed the successful application of terror makes further use for this function superfluous. In practice, of course, there is frequently "unnecessary" abuse in its application. Moreover, there may be no sharp distinction between this stage of power consolidation and the subsequent stage of development.

At that later stage systematic, purposive terror tends to become a dominant feature of the system: fear becomes an organizing principle of "permanent revolution" (to use Sigmund Neumann's phrase), of what social scientists have more recently labeled a mobilization system.[15] Here terror comes to serve the two major objectives of the regime: on the one hand, political *control*, with the elites typically striving for a monopoly of the instruments of control, and, on the other, *change*, with the Communist leadership characteristically attempting to carry out drastic transformations of the society, the economy, and the citizen.

The elite, committed as it is to substantial transformations—whether for ideological or for power-political reasons—is bound to encounter and generate resistance and alienation, since the changes it is determined to carry out will necessarily clash with the values and perceived interests of some significant sectors of society. Anticipating such hostility, the authorities, in line with their preconceptions and images of class or group loyalties and grievances, may identify certain strata as requiring preemptive, or prophylactic, suppression, intimidation, or removal. Typically such measures require the use of terror.

Communist regimes have characteristically moved to massive transformation programs, such as rapid industrialization and collectivization of agriculture, with intense commitment and short timetables. To secure the crucial "breakthrough" requires a mobilization and reallocation of human and natural resources

[15] The defining characteristics of a mobilization system are the acquisition by the state of control over all societal resources, human and economic, and the commitment of these assets to the attainment of a single, predominant goal. Since control can never be total, a mobilization system is an ideal-type model. See also the introductory chapter in Johnson, ed., *Change in Communist Systems*; and Herbert Spiro, "Totalitarianism," p. 111.

that will impose considerable strains and stresses on society and the economy. And, as Barrington Moore argues persuasively, everything else being equal, the more rapid and more extensive the change, the greater and more bitter the alienation. Organized terror now serves to ensure compliant behavior during such a period of change, and to this extent, political terror, however painful or distasteful, has a rational base.

Communist practice, however, has typically moved beyond these paroxysms of directed change, with total mobilization increasingly shaping the system. Most instances of massive political terror under Communism appear to have served the functions of destroying or inhibiting all rival authorities, and of insulating the population from all incongruent value systems. The net effect is to eliminate all organized political opposition and to facilitate socialization by exposing the population to a single, unchallenged system of values.[16]

But this process tends to have a dynamic of its own. Reaching beyond actually or possibly culpable individuals who become the victims of terror, the process begins to engulf entire social groups on the basis of "negative loyalty indicators" and automatic arrest categories. As Alfred Meyer has aptly remarked, this amounts to the bureaucratization of class warfare. In turn, from specific categories of "open enemies," whether real or imagined, it is extended to other sectors of society. But, whereas the Maoist strategy defines the "out-group"—those who, in Bolshevik jargon, are destined for the garbage heap of history—so narrowly as to leave open the possibility of reeducating most class-alien elements, the Stalinist variant is marked not only by an intense commitment to the pursuit of monolithic authority, the extermination of all autonomy of subgroups, and the suppression of all divided (or "unauthentic") allegiances, but also by a far narrower definition of the "in-group"—those who can be trusted as and those who can be made over into "good Communists." The momentum of political terror is thus further

---

[16] A related aspect is what has been labeled "a passion for unanimity." For an analysis of the multiple functions of unanimity and its various roots, see Edgar Schein et al., *Coercive Persuasion*, pp. 62–110.

increased by additional variables, such as the personality of dictators like Stalin.

Over time, however, the relative priority of the two objectives —control and change—tends to shift, and so does the place of political terror relative to other means that can serve the same functions. Finally, the more the regime succeeds in attaining its middle-range objectives, the more it generates forces that require systemic change. Particularly as a result of these un-intended consequences of economic growth and bureaucratiza-tion, the counterproductivity of political terror as an instrument of public policy becomes clearer as the system moves beyond its mobilization stage.

Thus, once the essential "breakthrough" is achieved, and once the regime gains wider legitimacy and succeeds in industrializ-ing the country, these three trends may be observed: (1) More reliance is placed on material incentives, as the regime has a greater total of utilitarian assets available to allocate; as effi-ciency criteria tend to acquire a greater value than was true at an earlier stage; as values change to accommodate vertical dif-ferentiation in status, income, and power; and as the standard of living rises so that the effective demand for material goods and services increases as part of the "revolution of rising expecta-tions." (2) Less reliance is placed on coercive power; terror, in particular, tends to be increasingly perceived by the elite as dysfunctional. Moreover, as considerations of rationality come to occupy a more prominent place, purposive terror will tend to be resisted more and more. In the end, the elite will no longer be willing to pay the price suggested in David Apter's formula that a high-coercion system is also a low-information system.[17] (3) Finally, as the regime gains widespread legitimacy, the ad-ministration becomes bureaucratized, and various mechanisms of socialization are routinized, the leadership can to a greater extent rely on — and, to an extent, manipulate — normative

---

[17] For an interesting discussion of the hypothesis that there exists an inverse relation-ship between coercion and information, see David Apter, *The Politics of Modernization*, pp. 40, 244, 398, 409, 421, 453–54.

power as well as administrative-bureaucratic procedures and communications, to secure control and compliance.

This stylized and oversimplified picture assumes that the manipulation of political control can be a rational process, with changes in instrumentalities and processes following changes in goals, available assets, and perceived priorities. To assert such an underlying regularity is not at all to deny that other variables —such as a given political culture, the psychology of an individual leader, intra-bloc and international relations—may intervene decisively to shape particular cases. But it does assume that significant deviations from the "ideal type" are explicable in terms of specific intervening variables in every case.

Terror: The Heritage

Governments have practiced political terror for thousands of years. Although its use varies with a given regime's capacity and willingness to employ it, it is safe to assume that any system and any people may experience political terror.[18] In general, as Robert Dahl has suggested, "the most commonplace way for a government to deal with its opponents is to employ violence."[19] In recent times violence has become increasingly disguised; however, political theorists have continued to debate whether coercion or consensus is at the base of power in organized societies.[20]

Karl Marx and the Communists after him follow in the tradition of those who see the state as organized force and, hence, as an instrumentality of coercion. To be sure, Marxism exhibits the well-known tension between the acceptance of violence as an inevitable concomitant of the class struggle and therefore of all class societies, past and present, on the one hand, and the utopia of a classless society in which all instruments of coercion would

---

[18] See Walter, *Terror and Resistance*, pp. vii, 3–4, 10 *et seq*.
[19] *Political Oppositions in Western Democracies*, pp. xi–xii. Dahl adds that an opposition is likely to be permitted and institutionalized if either of two conditions is met by a given polity: either the government believes that any attempt to coerce the opposition must fail; or even if it succeeded, the costs of coercion would exceed the gains.
[20] For a critical and original analysis, see Johnson, *Revolutionary Change*, pp. 16–39.

wither away, on the other. For the future, Marxism-Leninism
distinguishes between the "lower" stage of socialism, in which
organs of compulsion are needed, and the "higher" stage of Communism, in which coercive institutions are presumed to wither
as the population comes to share the values of the elite.

The ultimate goal of socialization for orthodox Communists
is, then, to have every citizen internalize all the prescribed goals
and values. Once this is achieved, each citizen will effortlessly
be a "good Communist." Thus the Communist approach to directed societal change reflects a fundamental assumption that
man's perfectability is unlimited and that the transformation of
the individual into a "new man" is both desirable and possible.

This doctrinal perspective is important not only in shaping
the Communist commitment to socioeconomic transformations
but also in providing a justification for the use of terror. As
early as 1904 Lenin was heard to declare, "The dictatorship of
the proletariat is an absolutely meaningless expression without
Jacobin coercion."[21] His later statements and writings abound
in such affirmations as "the scientific concept of dictatorship
means nothing else but power based directly on violence, unrestrained by any laws, absolutely unrestricted by any rules."
Soon after the seizure of power he reiterated that "it would be
madness to renounce coercion."[22] Violence and legality are but
alternative techniques of political control: law is conceived to
be, in Otto Kirchheimer's phrase, "the twin but respectable
brother of terror."[23] During the following months, Trotsky re-
called, "Lenin, at every passing opportunity, emphasized the
absolute necessity of terror."[24]

[21] Nikolai Valentinov, *Encounters with Lenin*, p. 128.
[22] Vladimir Lenin, *Polnoe sobranie sochinenii*, XLI, 383; XLII, 294. In his *State and
Revolution* (1917) Lenin approvingly cites Engels' "Anti-Dühring": the state is a "special repressive force." Hence, says Lenin, the task is to make it "a 'special repressive
force' of the proletariat for the suppression of the bourgeoisie."
[23] *Political Justice*, p. 287n.
[24] Lenin, pp. 133, 137. It should be noted, however, that some prominent Bolsheviks
protested the use of terror at an early date. Four members of the first Soviet government explained their resignation in a statement (endorsed by a number of other leaders) that pointed up the alternatives before the regime: either to broaden the composition of the government, or to "maintain a purely Bolshevik government by means of
political terror." Though the government had chosen to do the latter, "we cannot and
do not wish to do so. We see that this leads to . . . a regime of irresponsibility and to
the destruction of the revolution." (Miliutin, Nogin, Rykov, Teodorovich, and others,

Trotsky, in his polemic against Karl Kautsky, provided perhaps the most elaborate justification for the use of political terror, violence, and intimidation. "The man who repudiates terrorism in principle," he wrote in 1920, "i.e., repudiates measures of suppression and intimidation towards determined and armed counterrevolution, must reject all idea of the political supremacy of the working class and its revolutionary dictatorship." After providing a variety of examples in support of his argument that terror and violence have been characteristic of all revolutions, Trotsky concluded:

> The problem of revolution as of war consists in breaking the will of the foe, forcing him to capitulate and accept the conditions of the conqueror.... The question as to who is to rule ... will be decided on either side, not by references to the paragraphs of the constitution, but by the employment of all forms of violence.... War, like revolution, is founded upon intimidation. A victorious war generally destroys only an insignificant part of the conquered army, intimidating the remainder and breaking their will. The revolution works in the same way: it kills individuals and intimidates thousands.[25]

In the heroic days of War Communism, the Bolsheviks candidly acknowledged that they were engaged in Red Terror. Yet their initial assumption that they needed merely "to brush away the remnants of the old order,"[26] like so many others, proved naive. Just as "permanent revolution" took the place of "instant revolution," just as the transition from capitalism to Communism had to be stretched out in Communist doctrine from a moment to an ever-growing number of generations, so the continued use of force had to be justified, since total mobilization in the Stalinist view required the protracted use of terror too.[27]

"Zaiavlenie gruppy narodnykh komissarov," November 4 [17], 1917.) See also below, ch. 2, n. 10; and Boris Nicolaevsky, *Power and the Soviet Elite*, pp. 5, 18, 32ff.

[25] *Terrorism and Communism*, pp. 23, 51, 54–55, 58, 63.

[26] Moore, pp. 173 *et seq.*

[27] There are virtually no systematic or analytical discussions of the use of terror, especially in Communist systems, to be found in contemporary Communist writings. However, some suggestive comments appeared especially in the Khrushchev era, for example in connection with condemnations of Stalin, forecasts of the "new Soviet man," arguments for more material incentives and for extralegal "voluntary" organs of control. There has been little explicit treatment of this problem in East European publications. For the Chinese approach, see below, ch. 4. Although there remains a particular sensitivity to the public discussion of this and related matters in Communist systems, some "revisionist" spokesmen—Tito, Togliatti, Nagy, for example—felt obliged to speak out on them. So, of course, have a considerable number of ex-Communists.

But whereas Lenin had frankly explained the use of terror as a pragmatic response to threats from international capitalism, Stalin's justification was to be awkward and devious. By 1937, he had formulated the thesis that with the approach of the transition to full socialism, the class struggle was bound to sharpen further—a contrived rationale that his successors repudiated in 1956.[28]

[28] It is true that the core of Stalin's thesis was suggested by Trotsky as early as 1920. As he wrote in reply to Kautsky, "Under socialism there will not exist the apparatus of compulsion itself, namely, the state, for it will have melted away entirely. . . . Nonetheless, the road to socialism lies through a period of the highest intensification of the principle of the state." (Trotsky, *Terrorism and Communism*, pp. 169–70.) This dialectical approach has been partially revived in Brezhnev's argument (e.g., in his speech of June 7, 1969) that the higher the level of societal development the more difficult its tasks.

2 The Takeover Stage

Lenin: Do you really believe that we can be victorious without
the cruelest revolutionary terror?
I.N. Steinberg: Then why do we bother with a Commissariat of
Justice? Let's call it frankly the Commissariat for Social
Extermination and be done with it!
Lenin: Well put . . . that's exactly what it should be. . . . But we
can't say that.

After a Communist regime seizes central power, it tends to
resort to political terror as part of an effort to consolidate its
position. At this stage terror serves first to assure the survival of
the revolutionary regime and second to extend and tighten its
control. Its primary functions here are the elimination of pre-
revolutionary and other active adversaries by means other than
open combat and the deterrence of hostile acts by potential enemies. The use of terror at this stage seems more characteristic
of revolutionary regimes in general (whether in Russia, or in
the French Revolution, or in any other non-Communist revolutionary takeover) than the use of terror at the later, mobilization, stage. At least to begin with, terror seems to be viewed as
an extension of the "right" of self-defense and of open warfare
against internal and external foes. And characteristically for
Communist elites, the line between defense and offense tends
to be considered either purely technical and formal or else impossible to draw.

The experiences of Communist regimes at the takeover stage
fall into certain patterns that help explain variations in the
use of political terror. The type, scope, and effectiveness of terror at this stage appear to be related to at least four clusters of
variables: the "road to power," that is, the particular form of
gaining control of the instruments of national government; the
relative level of organizational control, including the strength
and scope of the Communists' organizational net relative to

that of their adversaries, the extent of their administrative penetration of the country, and the extent and viability of alternative organizations and authorities; the extent of societal disruption and exhaustion, including the relative propensity of the
population to accept *any* authoritative alternative to the status
quo, and the acuity of social tensions in the country; and the
nature of the dominant political culture—its attitude toward
violence, for example—and of the political strategy pursued by
the revolutionary elite (e.g., the championing of broad "multi-
class" alliances or national causes).

The process of coming to power has in practice been carried
out in three ways: the central government is seized by means
of a coup, and civil war ensues (Russia); power is gained by
armed struggle, from gradually expanding territorial bases
(China, Yugoslavia, Albania, Cuba, Vietnam); and Communist regimes are imposed (usually with an intermediate phase
of shared formal power) under varying circumstances that have
one overriding condition in common, the presence or threat
of external military force (most of Eastern Europe, as well as
Mongolia and North Korea).[1]

In virtually all cases, the takeover has come in the aftermath
of national crises—most frequently, war. The society in crisis
experiences a disruption of the old patterns of social roles and
expectations, magnifying tensions among classes, nationalities,
and political groups; most important, perhaps, organizational
structures previously deemed legitimate break down.[2]

Typically, the effort to take control of key institutions, such
as parliament, trade unions, and national administration, occurs
against a background of multivariate terror. The adversary may
use terror, either before or after the takeover: the "whites" did

---

[1] This typology deals only with the fourteen successful takeovers of national governments. For a comparative analysis, see Robert Tucker, "Paths of Communist Revolution,
1917–1967." See also Feliks Gross, *The Seizure of Political Power*.
[2] On the importance of the breakdown of old patterns as a precondition for authentic
revolutionary takeover, see, for example, Cyril Black, "The Anticipation of Communist Revolutions," pp. 425–27; R. V. Burks, "Eastern Europe"; Tucker, "Paths of
Communist Revolution," pp. 17ff; and Hugh Seton-Watson, *The East European Revolution*. For a psychoanalytic approach, see Gustav Bychowski, *Dictators and Disciples*,
p. 242.

in Russia, the Japanese in China, and the Germans in Eastern Europe. Spontaneous violence may occur under conditions of uncontrolled revolutionary chaos. "Controlled class warfare" such as was used in Russia and China, usually pitting the poor against the rich, especially in the countryside, may be stimulated and presumably contained by the new revolutionary regime. Finally, there may be organized institutional terror, either by traditional agencies such as the army (in China, and to some extent in Russia) or by newly created institutions (such as the Cheka in Russia and its various equivalents in Eastern Europe).

Although the revolutionary leadership may choose to provoke the adversary into escalating his terror (and examples abound, from Yugoslavia to Vietnam), in the hope of sharpening the cleavage and shaping popular loyalties in its own interest, basically terror by the adversary and spontaneous violence are not subject to Communist manipulation. It is the use of "controlled class warfare" and institutional terror that concerns us here. In the perception of Communist elites, terror may help achieve a variety of objectives, which may be ranked in the order of their importance to the regime. First in importance, the regime feels it necessary to eliminate those suspected of active hostility—the minimal goal being the survival of the regime, and its behavior being typically "reactive." Second, the regime is committed to deterring hostile action on the part of political opponents by intimidation, by demonstration of its superior force and the consequences of resistance, or by the destruction and discrediting of organized alternatives. Over the long haul such deterrence may be best assured by the reintegration of society and successful socialization, but in the early phases coercion is stressed. The role of indigenous agencies of deterrence may be taken over by external force (or the threat of external force): this was, of course, the role played by the Soviet army in much of Eastern Europe and in North Korea at the end of World War II. Third, the revolutionary regime seeks to extend its control across the country whose government is nominally in its hands. Fourth, it aims at the prophylactic elimination of potential opponents, as identified by the revolutionary elite either empirically or on the basis of ideological preconceptions. Fifth, it is committed to transforming the country's socioeconomic structure.

Political terror is one of the means by which these goals can be pursued. Its employment, then, varies with the priorities of the new regime.[3] And whereas the first and, to some extent, the second are essential to the survival and consolidation of power, the other objectives may be postponed to a later time.

Approaches to achieving these objectives have generally followed three patterns, depending largely on the degree of popular support a regime feels it has at takeover. If the central government is taken over before any of these objectives is substantially met, the new regime (as in Russia in 1917–18), once challenged, may feel obliged to try to eliminate active resistance. It may do this by systematic armed warfare (i.e. civil war, if the internal enemy has retained the ability to organize effectively as well as the will and the means to fight) and by the selective or demonstrative elimination of active opponents and opposition leaders (for example, in Russia, anarchist and "left Socialist-Revolutionary" militants and, in Eastern Europe, members of non-Communist home armies). Whereas the elimination of overt enemies by open warfare does not ordinarily involve political terror, the liquidation of opponents within the territory controlled by the new regime typically does. In Russia, this is what the Red Terror came to connote. In Poland, likewise, the Com-

[3] Among the many sources on terror in the takeover stage, see, for the Soviet Union: William Chamberlin, *The Russian Revolution*; E. H. Carr, *A History of Soviet Russia*; Leonard Schapiro, *The Origin of the Communist Autocracy*; Robert Slusser and Simon Wolin, eds., *The Soviet Secret Police*; Sergei Mel'gunov, *The Red Terror in Russia*; and I. N. Steinberg, *Gewalt und Terror in der Revolution* and *In the Workshop of the Revolution*. Among contemporary Soviet publications, see VCheKa, *Krasnaia Kniga*, I; Martin Latsis (pseud.), *Dva goda bor'by na vnutrennem fronte* and *Chrezvychainye Komissii*; among post-Stalin publications, see especially *Iz istorii Vserossiiskoi Chrezvychainoi Komissii 1917–1921 gg.; sbornik dokumentov*; and Pavel Sofinov, *Ocherki istorii VChK (1917–1922 gg.)*.

For Eastern Europe, see Brzezinski, *The Soviet Bloc*, and sources listed therein; Paul Kecskemeti, *The Unexpected Revolution*; Massachusetts Institute of Technology, CENIS, series of papers, "The Soviet Takeover of Eastern Europe"; Richard Medalie, "The Policy of Takeover: The Stages of Totalitarian Development in Eastern Europe"; Paul Zinner, *Communist Strategy and Tactics in Czechoslovakia*.

For China, see Johnson, *Peasant Nationalism and Communist Power*; Doak Barnett, *China on the Eve of Communist Takeover* and *Communist China: The Early Years*.

munists assumed the formal reins of power at the end of World War II before the organized strength of other political groups was neutralized. The Soviet presence made up for the weakness of Polish Communist organizations (and made civil warfare impossible for the regime's opponents), but the new leadership nonetheless required substantial violence—including terror—to eliminate political resistance. In Cuba, too, political terror was used for the liquidation of hostile groups and authorities.[4]

If, on the other hand, prior to the takeover of the central government the revolutionary movement is successful in gaining a fair measure of popular support, in penetrating the administrative-organizational system of the country, and in gaining the upper hand over alternative organizations and authorities—whether by guerrilla warfare against domestic or foreign enemies (China, Yugoslavia, Albania) or by administrative manipulation, through front organizations, party and police operations, or other backstage moves (Czechoslovakia, Hungary)—then there is correspondingly less "need" for terror (and no civil war) after the takeover of the central government. The equivalent functions of terror at this stage will have been substantially fulfilled prior to takeover.

If, finally, the revolutionary regime believes it can or needs to take advantage of the fluidity of the takeover stage to move on to the extension of its control or to the prophylactic elimination of potential opponents, however it may define them, it may embark on any one or more of further actions that typically require the use of political terror. It may make a synthetic effort to replicate the revolutionary cycle of destroying traditional authorities at the local level and replacing them with Communist authorities (China). It may carry out "controlled class warfare" against social groups ideologically defined as class enemies (Russia, China). It may selectively eliminate potential opposition leaders through political and secret-police operations (most of Eastern Europe).

[4] See Theodore Draper, *Castroism, Theory and Practice*; and Inter-American Commission on Human Rights, *Report on the Situation of Political Prisoners and Their Relatives in Cuba*.

The differential impact of organizational control by the Communist regime is related to the nature of the objectives it chooses to pursue at this stage. If its short-range goal is to eliminate and deter active resistance, terror tends to be inversely related to its level of organizational control, everything else being equal. Thus, in Russia the Bolsheviks were at the time of their takeover a relatively small group that assumed power before effectively penetrating the country administratively and before eliminating anti-Communist authorities and organizations. They therefore found themselves soon obliged to fight a civil war, to seek to eliminate active opponents—usually by overt terror—and also to destroy or neutralize the influence of prerevolutionary authorities, such as pre-Communist officials, the landed gentry, the clergy, and the "bourgeoisie," largely by means of class warfare. Similarly, in Poland the organizational control of the new regime was relatively low, even with the presence of Soviet armed forces and police agents. Hence, once again, a substantial amount of terror was required to achieve the minimum objective of political survival, the precondition for further consolidation and control.

On the other hand, substantially less political terror was used or generated in Czechoslovakia at the takeover stage. Here the indigenous Communist organization was comparatively strong and had fairly extensive popular support, and the formal takeover in February 1948 was the culmination of a process during which the ruling party had managed to extend its influence and control across the country. No organized political rivals remained who could have mounted any effective resistance. With the greater power and authority of the new regime (and the shadow of the Red Army) acting as a deterrent to political deviance, terror subsequent to the seizure of power could for the moment be applied sparingly and selectively.

In Hungary, too, the formal takeover did not come until after the will and ability to resist of oppositional organizations had been gradually broken. In this case, the weakness of the Communist party and its organization was compensated for by the organizational control exercised by the Soviet armed forces, which performed the equivalent deterrent function. Purposive terror at this stage was essentially limited to the selective elimination of active political opponents and representatives of pre-revolutionary elites, with the "demonstration effect" aimed at broader strata of the population as yet distinctly subordinate.[5]

In China and Yugoslavia, the road to power led through protracted armed warfare, involving the sustained expansion of a highly disciplined administrative-revolutionary organization. Both revolutionary elites engaged in "agitational terror"[6] against the foreign occupiers, often provoking brutal repression that in turn drove the population into the arms of the Communists as the most stable, best organized, and, moreover, indigenous authority. Here the Communists stood for an alternative social order, championing the national cause even before assuming central power, in a context of disintegrating social patterns and keenly perceived threats from the outside.

Under the circumstances, alternative indigenous authorities proved to be relatively ineffective. Any potential resistance that remained at the end of the stage of open warfare was fairly easily neutralized. In China effective intimidation, largely by the victorious army, made wanton terror relatively unnecessary for the consolidation of power. It is noteworthy, however, that in the Chinese case the regime was not content with the attainment of minimum objectives. Compared to other takeover regimes the Chinese Communists characteristically expended more of their coercive resources in the pursuit of less urgent goals: even if the organizational net was relatively strong, the additional liquidation, mobilization, or transformation functions could be served by the use of terror. The Chinese leadership used "con-

[5] We distinguish between "purposive terror," which is initiated and intended by the policy-makers, and "situational terror," which is generally a product of uncontrolled and undisciplined behavior by lower-level cadres.
[6] On "agitational terror," see Thornton, "Terror as a Weapon of Political Agitation." Ernst Halperin indirectly corroborates our argument by concluding in The Triumphant Heretic, p. 30, that in Yugoslavia terror in the consolidation phase was nonreactive, not intended to "break the backbone of an opposition" or to "punish the sins of collaborators." Rather, he interprets it as a tool of demographic and social revolution: smash the old economic and administrative system, remove old public servants, and replace them with "partisans from the mountains."

trolled class warfare" following the formal conquest of the
mainland in 1949 to extend its administrative and political
sway, especially to remote areas of the country. Here—suggestive
of "permanent revolution," perhaps—the takeover stage grew
into the mobilization stage, with terror being applied selectively, against landlords for example, not so much to get rid
of them as to demonstrate their frailty to the tradition-bound
villagers.[7]

The existence of acute social tensions in the takeover stage
was a necessary condition for successful "controlled class warfare" as Russia and China demonstrate, but it was not a sufficient condition. In Hungary, for instance, no such campaign
was undertaken despite the presence of social tensions. And the
disruption of prior patterns was one important determinant of
the ease with which the population could then be mobilized by
the revolutionary regime. Still, despite the presence of both
conditions, purposive class warfare was evidently required for
the breakdown of traditional authority patterns in China, presumably because traditional patterns and expectations were so
profoundly ingrained.

In general, more extensive or intensive coercion is called for
if the regime seeks to pursue several objectives simultaneously.
Thus, in Russia the struggle for power coincided with the
attempt to extend Communist primacy, if not yet to the point
of complete control then at least to the point of deterring the
population from joining the "whites." Here the problem was
further complicated by the situational terror generated among
parts of the rural population as an unintended but predictable
by-product of the Bolsheviks' ruthless requisition of produce.
Furthermore, when the relative level of Bolshevik organizational development was still quite low, especially in the rural
areas, the need to fight a civil war made it inevitable that much
terror would be caused by undisciplined, zealous, or stupid officials, by graft, accidents, and bureaucratic failures of communication.

[7] See below, pp. 62–63.

Under some circumstances, a regime chooses to embark on the prompt pursuit of several diverse uses of terror. For instance, at the time of the Soviet takeover of eastern Poland and the Baltic States in 1939–41, the military occupation and relative insulation from the outside world made possible (and the urgency of the situation appeared to make necessary, at least to the Soviet authorities) a telescoping of terror campaigns that manifested the typical functions of both the takeover and the mobilization stages.[8]

There appear to be built-in elements that lead Communist regimes to limit the use of political terror at the takeover stage. There is, first of all, the ubiquitous concern of modern mass movements—however paradoxical it may seem in the case of "totalitarian" ones—about their legitimacy and popular support. As one student of Communist strategies of revolution has remarked, "While violence may dominate the process of the transfer of power, it may—indeed it should—be substituted for by methods short of violence whenever this is possible."[9] Behind this view lies an awareness that terror, if applied "excessively" or, from the viewpoint of the policy-maker, "indiscriminately," can prove counterproductive by dint of its negative impact on popular support. This was implicit in the shift away from terror decreed by the Soviet leadership toward the end of the civil war.[10]

---

[8] See the "top secret" documents relating to the activity of the NKGB in the Baltic States in 1940–41, reproduced in *Lithuanian Bulletin*. The instructions provide for statistical information on specified categories "regardless of the existence of concrete data on their anti-Soviet activity at the present time" and their subsequent removal from the Baltic states. The categories include 26 groups of former Lithuanian officials and social groups, as well as various "counterrevolutionary," nationalist, and emigré groups. (*Lithuanian Bulletin*, III: 5 [1945], 21–24. See also Deputy Commissar of the NKGB USSR, Serov, "Instruktsiia o poriadke provedeniia operatsii po vyseleniiu antisovetskogo elementa iz Litvy, Latvii i Estonii," in *ibid.*, IV: 1 [1946], 18–35; and "Prikaz NKGB LSSR No. 0023 za 1941 g.," in *ibid.*, IV: 3 [1946], 24–31.)

[9] Andrew Janos, "The Communist Theory of the State and Revolution," p. 37. See also Gross, *The Seizure of Political Power*, p. 35: "The concept of legitimacy forms a part of the philosophy of transfer of power."

[10] In mid-1918, after the assassination of several Bolshevik leaders and the attempt on Lenin's life, Soviet authorities called for tenfold retribution for every anti-Soviet act. Trotsky declared, "We shall not enter the kingdom of socialism in white gloves on a polished floor." Feliks Dzerzhinski, head of the Cheka, proclaimed that it was the duty of his agency to "defend the revolution . . . even if its sword happens to strike the

Finally, in Soviet-controlled Eastern Europe some restraint in the use of political terror at the takeover stage must be ascribed to the techniques of Stalinist "dosage." The calculated tolerance of a measure of "domesticism" and residual pluralism implied a postponement, if only for a short time, of an all-out drive against political opponents and potential enemies.[11]

But of course the decisive circumstance making terror self-terminating—for *these* objectives and at *this* stage—is usually the successful elimination or neutralization of effective resistance. Sooner or later all surviving Communist regimes attain this goal. Such success may be deceptive, for it conceals unintended consequences of the use of terror. In addition to the alienating and economically disruptive outcomes noted above, it provides a precedent that—especially in the context of the characteristic Communist justification by precedent or authority—tends to provide *a priori* a blanket justification, for the insiders at least, of subsequent terror, establishing what Crane

---

heads of innocent men." By contrast, in 1920 Lenin called for a change in tactics and in the character of repression appropriate to the shift from war to peace; and Dzerzhinski then declared that "at present" terror was not needed, for "the proletariat takes up this weapon only when it cannot do without it." Note that both Lenin and Dzerzhinski implied that terror was used out of weakness, not strength. See Borys Lewytzkyj, *Vom roten Terror zur sozialistischen Gesetzlichkeit*, pp. 26–43; and Konstantin Shteppa, "Feliks Dzerzhinski," in Slusser and Wolin, pp. 77–78.

It is interesting to note that there were serious differences and some ambiguity within the Bolshevik leadership with regard to the necessity and propriety of extreme terror in 1918–20 (e.g., with regard to the shooting of hostages). Some party members were concerned about the abuse, "insolence," and "contempt for the impotent" on the part of Cheka personnel, which they believed tarnished the reputation of all Bolsheviks. Others were fearful of the de facto immunity of the Cheka from party control, which might lead to a situation in which "the slogan, 'All power to the soviets' is replaced by the slogan, 'All power to the Cheka.'" Lenin at times reproved his associates for undue "liberalizing," while at other times he charged Cheka personnel with "scandalously" undisciplined behavior. The extreme attitude, according to which "some men are held responsible for the deeds of others," was epitomized by the injunction of Martin Latsis, a leading Cheka official, "Do not seek in your accusations proof of whether the prisoner has rebelled against the soviets with guns or by word. You must ask him, first, what class he belongs to, what his social origin is, what his education was, and his profession. The answers must determine the fate of the accused. That is the meaning of Red Terror." (Latsis, "Zakony grazhdanskoi voiny ne pisany.") Dzerzhinski in his order of January 8, 1921, barred the use of "crude criteria" of collective guilt (e.g., against kulaks, gentry, and tsarist officers) in favor of evidence of individual culpability.

11 See Brzezinski, *The Soviet Bloc*, ch. 3; Burks, "Eastern Europe," p. 101; Zinner, *Communist Strategy and Tactics in Czechoslovakia*, p. 121: "Caution and moderation in varying degrees characterized the actions of all East European parties in this period." Another source of self-limitation in resorting to terror must be sought in the particular political culture of certain societies. On the greater commitment of the Chinese Communists to "voluntarist" techniques and the combination of coercive with normative uses, see below, ch. 4.

Brinton has labeled a "habit of violence" as a characteristic style of Communist regimes.

Moreover, it brings into being the nucleus of institutions that have henceforth a vested interest in their self-perpetuation and expansion of functions: the secret police—or, in the case of China, the police and the revolutionary army—becomes a special interest group with dynamics of its own that may or may not prove functional for the system.[12]

[12] See Frederick Barghoorn, "The Security Police"; and Lewytzkyj, *Die rote Inquisition.* On the Chinese People's Liberation Army, see John Gittings, *The Role of the Chinese Army.*

3 The Mobilization Stage: Control Functions

> Look at this city
> Its prisons are crowded
> With our friends. . . .
> They all stand huddled together there
> and hear through the windows
> the guards talking about executions
> Now they talk of people as gardeners talk
>   of leaves for burning
> Their names are crossed off the top of a list
> and as the list grows shorter
> more names are added at the bottom.
>   *Charlotte Corday, in Peter Weiss*, Marat/Sade

Mobilization entails the acquisition of control by the state over the resources within the society; by the "mobilization stage," however, we mean the stage in which the Communist regime attempts to score a decisive breakthrough[1] toward one or more critical goals, such as industrialization, by investing all the needed resources for this purpose at the expense of other goals and needs. The process of mobilization then becomes a central means toward this end.[2] As a result, political controls at this stage are extended to cover the entire society—all its members and all its associations. Purposive political terror now primarily serves the two functions of eliminating rival authority figures—

---

[1] A "breakthrough" refers to the process by which an elite overcomes restraints on its ability to implement a program of revolutionary change. See Otto Kirchheimer, "Confining Conditions and Revolutionary Breakthroughs." A more specific definition speaks of it as "a process designed to alter or destroy values, structures, and behaviors which are perceived by a revolutionary elite as comprising or contributing to the actual or potential existence of alternative centers of political power." Kenneth Jowitt, "A Comparative Analysis of Leninist and Nationalist Elite Ideologies and Nation-Building Strategies," p. 1.

[2] The distinction between a "mobilization system" and the "mobilization stage" should be borne in mind. The former is, as noted, an ideal-type model; the latter refers to a period in the history of Communist states. The stages we refer to thus amount to a taxonomy of periods in Communist development, identified by the processes dominant in each stage.

Industrialization need not be the only goal of such mobilization. Thus, China would properly be considered in its "mobilization stage" even if the transformation of values has, to its leaders, priority over industrialization.

actual, potential, or imagined—as well as their sub-elites, disciples, and subordinate bureaucracies; and eliminating incongruent value structures, either by neutralizing or removing groups identified *a priori* as carriers of such values, or else by isolating the population from access to them.

Although the two functions are not always clearly separable, they involve different processes. The former tends to take the form of "purges,"[3] whereas the latter may involve the removal or repression of authoritative individuals who neither are, nor are likely to become, political challengers, and of entire socioeconomic, ethnic, religious, or other groups and demographic categories identified by "objective characteristics" as bad risks, or the elimination of certain quotas of individuals within such groups. Either process may be "hermetic" or may include deterrent purposes and "demonstration" effects—the latter being typically absent when publicity of a given group's removal or victimization is politically or ideologically compromising for the regime.

What the two functions have in common is the characteristic attempt to deny the viability of any alternatives to the regime's monopoly over the two central objects of Leninist concern: organization (authority) and ideology (values). One may, it is true, conceive of Communist systems that would not exhibit these characteristics; indeed, there are clearly variations in the degree of commitment to them.[4] Yet in the Soviet experience, which, after all, was prototypical and was subsequently transferred to other Communist polities, the striving for a monopoly in these areas—including maximal central control and the elimination of all autonomous subgroups within the system—is an integral part of the operational code.

This "passion for unanimity" follows from the commitment to a single belief system and a single hierarchy, the practical ex-

---

[3] Purges may, but need not, involve the use of terror. Bureaucratic purges, for instance, do not require severe coercion; neither does the periodic purge of party membership.

[4] Thus, Maoism lacks the hysterical antispontaneity animus of Soviet Communism; and Titoism soon shed the Bolshevik commitment to total centralization of control.

pression of which includes the attempt to control the citizen's behavior by leaving him no viable alternative but to comply. As Bauer and Inkeles observe with regard to the Stalin era, it was "a cardinal point of policy to structure the individual's life situation so that choice situations occurred as seldom as possible."[5] Terror campaigns are among the means used to achieve this end.[6]

Our definition of terror stresses the element of arbitrariness both in the decision-maker's ability to disregard any binding legal norms and in the incalculability of the application of terror as perceived by the citizen. This second characteristic must not be confused, however, with capriciousness in the identification of victims. Whereas terror may come to affect any member of society either as victim or as target, it appears that in Communist systems neither the entire society is the primary target of terror campaigns, nor is terror randomly applied. And where the prophylactic removal of entire categories is involved, such groups—though not necessarily the individual victims within them—tend to be chosen for selective or total elimination by a rational, albeit peculiar, process.[7]

Whereas the outlines of the policy are rational, there is a frequent spillover of victimization beyond the confines of the original group of intended victims. Memoir literature from Russia, Eastern Europe, and China abounds in examples of individuals being implicated because of denunciations by opportunists, the mention of their names by suspects forced to confess to imaginary crimes, the accidental assumption of guilt-by-association, or the "snowballing" of purges and persecutions

[5] *The Soviet Citizen*, p. 283. It is this, presumably, that Karl Deutsch had in mind in citing the *bon mot* that "in a democracy everything that is not forbidden is permitted; under an authoritarian regime, everything that is not permitted is forbidden; under totalitarianism, everything that is not forbidden is compulsory." (Friedrich, ed., *Totalitarianism*, p. 309.)

[6] The attention paid to specific "campaigns" or "actions" is not meant to minimize the possible continuity and intensity of diffuse, "intransitive" terror, regardless of particular operations. Typically, such campaigns come at the "hard" peaks of alternating phases of militancy and moderation. For the argument that the origin of these zigzags is to be sought in the tension between the need for efficiency and the need for dynamism, which in turn stimulates and limits the use of coercive power, see Brzezinski, *The Permanent Purge*, pp. 19–20.

[7] By "rational" we mean here that there was a rough proportionality between ends (insulation from incongruent values) and means (the choice of categories of victims), given the policy-maker's perception of these groups as potential sources of dissent.

by eager security personnel who manufacture "guilt" criteria and espouse success standards of their own.[8] In practice, then, there is often an overlay of accidental and irrational elements making for the escalation of terror operations that in their conception and from the particular perspective of their sponsors might have been rational.

It must be acknowledged that we have no adequate means by which to determine just what elements in the record of the Stalin era represent something approximating an "ideal type" of a Communist polity at the mobilization stage and what other elements are but the manifestation of a peculiar and perhaps unique set of intervening variables, among which the dictator's personality by no means may be the least. In any event, it is appropriate to think of the variety of Communist experiences in a state of "general societal mobilization" (Etzioni's phrase) as being located on a spectrum whose polar positions are ultimate totalitarian degeneration, in which total control is an end in itself, and a rational process, in which the mobilization of coercive assets involves the liquidation of actual enemies and the prophylactic elimination of potential ones, however defined; in which the mobilization of material assets includes the repression of hostile classes and socioeconomic strata, such as landlords and kulaks; and in which the mobilization of normative assets (resocialization of the population) requires the denial of access to, or the removal of the sources of, competing values. We shall now discuss the mobilization of coercive and normative assets, leaving consideration of the mobilization of material resources for Chapter 5.

Terror Against Authority Figures

Although in the takeover stage the brunt of political terror is directed primarily against members of various "out-groups,"

[8] Even some of the most prominent victims of Communist terror were evidently implicated in such a fashion. For instance, according to a well-documented account, the arrest and judicial murder of Rudolf Slánský, one-time Secretary-General of the Communist Party of Czechoslovakia, was first vetoed on grounds of insufficient evidence and then acquiesced in by Stalin after strenuous work by Soviet secret-police personnel operating without the prior approval of Gottwald. See Karel Kaplan, "Zamyšlení nad politickými procesy," *Nová Mysl*; and *Život Strany*.

at the mobilization stage it also turns against insiders. The Soviet state after World War I, and the East European Communist states after World War II, experienced a succession of political terror campaigns remarkably similar in some of the categories of intended victims and some of the techniques applied. The typical pattern is a sequence of victimization beginning with active enemies and moving to erstwhile partners of the ruling party, to quasi-legal opponents from the "bourgeois" and "petty-bourgeois" camp, and finally to members of the Communist party, state, military, and police hierarchies.[9] At the mobilization stage, these last groups join the list of victims.

The outstanding and in some respects unique exhibit of a terror campaign whose primary function was the elimination of those whom the leader chose to single out as potential rivals or threats was the Great Purge, which Soviet society experienced in 1935–39 and in which the terror appears to have been particularly traumatic and pervasive. It cannot be our task here to examine in detail how and why the victims were chosen, why they confessed, or what accounts for the particular combination of methods employed in their elimination. That complex of trials and terror included, of course, the "show trials" of 1936–38, in which the most prominent surviving Bolsheviks[10] pleaded guilty to preposterous charges of treason and subversion; as well as trials in camera, for example of Marshal Tukhachevsky and other senior military commanders; liquidation without public announcement, usually after sentencing by a Special Board of the NKVD, including among its victims officials as high as members of the Politburo; clandestine murder; and deportation and exile for various terms, including massive internment in forced labor camps.[11]

[9] This sequence does not consider the victims of "transformation" terror, which is discussed in ch. 5, below.

[10] As Tucker correctly notes, Lenin's "Testament" singled out (in addition to Stalin, whose removal he recommended) five possible leaders: Trotsky, Zinovyev, Kamenev, Bukharin, and Pyatakov. Of these, Trotsky was condemned in absentia and assassinated by a Soviet agent in Mexico. All four others were among the victims of the Moscow Trials.

[11] On the Great Purge (and in some instances Soviet terror in general), see, for example, the works of Brzezinski, Fainsod, Lewytzkyj, Moore, and Slusser and Wolin, cited earlier; and Robert Conquest, *The Great Terror*; F. Beck and W. Godin (pseuds.),

The total scope of these purges, which soon touched off an avalanche of subsidiary but numerically far more extensive terror operations across the land, remains unknowable, but some magnitude of the victimization is suggested by the official Soviet admission, a generation later, that between the Seventeenth and Eighteenth Party Congresses (1934 and 1939) more than two-thirds of the members of the Central Committee (98 out of 139) were liquidated and about half the officers' corps (about 35,000 officers) were arrested, and by the various serious but highly speculative estimates that the number of people arrested at some time during the Great Purge may have been in the vicinity of seven million.[12]

And 1939 did not mark the end of such terror. Sentencing, executions, arrests, and accusations continued for the remainder of the Stalin era, though the later terror tended to be less sweeping, more controlled, more individual, and more diverse in character.[13] Moreover, it is clear that on the eve of his death in March 1953 Stalin was readying another major round of purges for totally fictitious crimes, of which the alleged "Doctors' Plot" to poison Soviet leaders was only the beginning.[14]

During the period of stringent Soviet control, the Communist leaders of Eastern Europe exhibited a similar tendency to eliminate rival authority figures, by terror if need be. But here the

---

Russian Purge and the Extraction of Confession; Boris Nicolaevsky, *Power and the Soviet Elite;* Werner Scharndorff, *Moskaus permanente Säuberung;* Tucker, "Introduction," to Tucker and Cohen, *The Great Purge Trial;* Alec Nove, *Economic Rationality and Soviet Politics.* For a somewhat divergent but sophisticated approach, see Maurice Merleau-Ponty, *Humanism and Terror.*

For additional memoirs and documents of particular interest, see Alexander Weissberg, *The Accused;* Eugenia Ginzburg, *Journey into the Whirlwind;* Ilya Ehrenburg, *Memoirs, 1921–1941;* Alexander Gorbatov, *Years Off My Life;* Seweryn Bialer, ed., *Stalin and His Generals;* Fainsod, *Smolensk Under Soviet Rule;* Alexander Orlov, *The Secret History of Stalin's Crimes;* and Khrushchev's "secret" speech at the Twentieth Party Congress, available in various editions, for example *The Anti-Stalin Campaign and International Communism.*

For fictional accounts of particular insight, see, for example, Arthur Koestler's *Darkness at Noon;* Alexander Solzhenitsyn's *The First Circle;* and Lydia Chukovskaya's *The Deserted House.*

[12] See Khrushchev's "secret" speech, in *The Anti-Stalin Campaign;* and Conquest, *The Great Terror,* in particular the Epilogue and Appendix A.

[13] But see Boris D'iakov, *Povest' o perezhitom,* as an example of Soviet memoirs relating the experiences of intellectuals and officials arrested in 1949–51, in Soviet prisons and labor camps.

[14] See Conquest, *Power and Policy in the USSR;* and Wolfgang Leonhard, *The Kremlin After Stalin.*

process was more compressed in time and occurred sooner after the takeover than it had in the Soviet Union. It thus tended to be less sweeping, the ruling parties tended to be less homogeneous and their leadership less skillful, and the purge remained uncompleted because of forces external to the polities involved. To a great extent, the similarities to the Soviet experience were acquired characteristics—thanks in part to the role of Soviet "security" advisers and Soviet "know-how." Indeed, the various security apparatuses within Eastern Europe were well coordinated and tended to disregard constraints traditionally imposed by national boundaries.[15] Moreover, many of the victims were implicated not for domestic reasons per se but because of their international ties (for example, they may have been former members of the International Brigades in Spain) or by analogy with the Soviet "line" (for example, "Zionist agents").

Still, there were significant differences from country to country. Whereas the Kostov trial in Bulgaria, the Rajk trial in Hungary, and the Slánský trial in Czechoslovakia outwardly followed the Soviet prototype closely, the Polish leadership managed to resist Soviet pressure to stage a similar show trial, and East Germany avoided it presumably with Soviet consent. In Eastern Europe the most sweeping terror was applied in the aftermath of Yugoslavia's defiance of the Soviet leadership in 1948, and the ensuing "anti-Titoist" campaign had all the earmarks of the Soviet purges: false confessions, the construction of elaborate and fictitious conspiracies, numerous arrests, and prison terms and executions, with or without publicity. Some of the victims had no "objective" reason to expect to be persecuted as real or potential Titoists (this is true, for instance, of László

---

[15] Such coordination is exemplified by the case of Noel, Herta, and Herman Field. Noel and Herta were arrested in Prague, shipped to and tried in Budapest; Herman was arrested in Warsaw (and Swiatlo, who handled his case, then went to Budapest to interrogate the Fields there); Erica Wallach, Noel's step-daughter, was arrested in East Berlin a year later and sent off to a Soviet labor camp. (See Flora Lewis, *Red Pawn: The Story of Noel Field*; and Erica Wallach, *Light at Midnight*.) For a first-hand account of the coordination of security services, on the basis of the Polish experience, see Józef Swiatlo, *Behind the Scene of the Party and Bezpieka*. Also see the transcript of the Eighth Plenum of the PZPR Central Committee, in *Nowe Drogi* (Warsaw), 10 (1956), 88.

Rajk), but a variety of pressures made for ever-widening circles of victims. Moscow's commitment to the extirpation of autonomous tendencies even beyond Soviet borders and the belief of some of the surviving members of the local elite that their purposes were served by the terror and the creation of a more monolithic apparat were two such pressures.[16]

By contrast, the record of the Chinese revolution until 1966 shows very little use of terror against rivals within the elite. Only two operations seem to qualify—the ouster of Kao Kang and Jao Shu-shih in 1954–55, and the removal of Marshal P'eng Te-huai in 1959—and in both instances real and serious policy differences were involved. These cases thus correspond more closely to the pattern of factional conflicts than to the contrived and prophylactic strikes that characterized the Soviet and East European purges. Even in these two instances, the ouster of deviationists within the party evidently led neither to physical extermination (though Kao did commit suicide and Jao's whereabouts are unknown) nor to an extensive witchhunt against their subordinates.[17]

Why was Soviet-type terror against rival members of the elite absent in China? Three possible explanations come to mind: the absence for many years—perhaps until 1958—of serious elite conflicts; a commitment, even on the part of Mao Tse-tung, to party solidarity, which served to prevent the perception of potential threats from rival authority figures, especially in the

---

[16] On Eastern Europe, see Brzezinski, *The Soviet Bloc*; Kecskemeti, *The Unexpected Revolution*; Paul Ignotus, *Political Prisoner*; Josefa Slánský, *Report on My Husband*; Hugo Dewar, *The Modern Inquisition*; Ghiţa Ionescu, *Communism in Rumania*; Vladimir Dedijer, *Tito*; William Griffith, ed., *Albania and the Sino-Soviet Rift*, and *European Communism*; Mordekhai Oren, *Prisonnier politique à Prague*; Paul Zinner, *Revolution in Hungary*; Eugen Loebl, *Stalinism in Prague*; Artur London, *L'aveu*; Vincent Savarius (pseud.), *Freiwillige für den Galgen*; Ernst Richert, *Macht ohne Mandat*, ch. 9. For a review of recent memoirs and documentary publications from Czechoslovakia, see Otto Ulč, "Koestler Revisited."

A study based on Czechoslovak party archives purports to show that, although some of the professed support of the terror in 1949–53 was contrived and manipulated, some Communist cadres welcomed the purges and trials because they provided scapegoats for failure that averted a crisis of confidence among men who had earlier nourished high hopes but now perceived an unhappy present and felt uncertain about the future. (V. Brabec, "The Relationship of the CPCS and the Public to the Political Trials of the Early Fifties.")

[17] On the Kao–Jao affair, see, for example, Barnett, *Communist China: The Early Years*, ch. 20; on the P'eng affair, see David A. Charles (pseud.), "The Dismissal of Marshal P'eng Teh-huai"; and J. D. Simmonds, "P'eng Te-huai: A Chronological Reexamination."

1950's; and Mao's sense of such weakness of his position within the leadership as to deter him from risking to purge real or potential rivals or to make him unwilling to test his authority by means of such a purge—perhaps after 1962. But an adequate explanation must also recognize the distinct political culture and revolutionary experience that helped shape the values and expectations of the Chinese elite.

It was only in 1966–68 that China experienced a combination of bitter and violent conflicts that, in terms of terror, broke with this tradition. We will not assign weights to the various contributing causes of these conflicts—Mao's determination to combat bureaucratization and loss of commitment in the ruling party; his attempt to insure the dominance of utopian over developmental goals; his desire to purge those who, he feared, might eventually challenge Maoism. In any event the Cultural Revolution ushered in mass violence and terror on many levels.[18]

The Struggle Against Incongruence

Acts of political terror that serve primarily to isolate or remove individuals and groups whose values and attitudes don't "fit" the desired loyalty profile of the leadership constitute a distinct category. Here the victims may be individuals who as writers, teachers, or performing artists, for instance, disseminate values deemed to be significantly and dangerously at variance with the official ones, and whose silencing or elimination could be expected to have a deterrent effect on other, potentially deviant, citizens.[19] More significant and more unique is the col-

---

[18] See below, pp. 57–60, where we review this in a different context.

In the case of Cuba, the elimination of rival authority figures and their subordinates does indeed seem to have been at the root of Fidel Castro's drive against the "old communists" during the first decade of power, culminating in the conviction of the group around Aníbal Escalante, one-time Secretary-General of the Cuban Communist Party, in early 1968. Here too terror seems to have been the ultimate expression of genuine differences, rather than a prophylactic or a deterrent operation. See Andrés Suárez, *Cuba: Castroism and Communism, 1959–1966*; and Kevin Devlin, "The Permanent Revolution of Fidel Castro."

[19] Individual cases, with broad terror consequences, date back to Soviet attempts to prosecute leading figures of the Russian Orthodox Church in the 1920's as part of the "militant atheism" campaign. In the case of figures such as Cardinal Mindszenty the purpose included the "demonstration" of subversive activities instigated by the Vatican. More directly exemplifying the category here under discussion are the various forms of intimidation and persecution of ostensibly "bourgeois-nationalist" figures from among the non-Russian nationalities of the Soviet Union; the public attack on, or ostracism of,

lective identification of entire groups on the basis of formal "objective characteristics" as subject to social or political prophylaxis.

The rather unusual process involved in the application of terror against members of such suspect groups is based on the assumption that any member of such a group is "objectively" prone to espousing deviant attitudes that would make him less than loyal. What this category has in common with the "show trials" is the victims' assumed culpability of potential crimes, not of offenses actually committed, despite the frequent manufacture of a fictitious case. As an astute observer and former victim of the Hungarian purges remarked in explaining why Imre Nagy survived the Stalin era and László Rajk did not, "the reason lay in the Communist mind. Assumable and potential deeds were more important than those which had been committed."[20]

One of the first students of "social prophylaxis" (himself an erstwhile inmate of Soviet labor camps) has listed the major categories from which groups are typically selected for such treatment:

(1) social class and class of origin: classes and strata considered to be inimical, either by doctrine or by plausibility;

(2) political affiliates: former members of non-Communist parties, and members of oppositionist and deviationist factions within the Communist party;

(3) persons with foreign contacts, suspect either for "security" reasons or for fear of contamination of ideas;

(4) ethnic groups: residents deported from Soviet border areas (Koreans, Poles, Finns) before World War II and from newly occupied territories (in 1939–41 and in 1944–46); nationalities punitively deported and deprived of territorial autonomy for (actual or anticipated) disloyalty during the war; and anti-Semitic aspects of post-1945 terror in the Soviet Union;

(5) persons with family ties, or close acquaintance, with other vic-

---

writers and scholars accused of Western sympathies, "cosmopolitanism," or otherwise failing to follow the official line. (On the purge of anti-Lysenkoists, see Zhores Medvedev, *The Rise and Fall of T. D. Lysenko*.) In China, the Cultural Revolution witnessed considerable, though evidently not centrally controlled, terror against persons accused of bourgeois tastes and habits (down to the wearing of jewelry and the keeping of pets).

[20] Ignotus, *Political Prisoner*, p. 60. He adds other reasons as well: "Personal jealousy was weightier than political disagreement. . . . Besides, Rákosi did not fear Nagy as a rival." Moreover, unlike Rajk, Nagy had returned to Hungary from Moscow.

tims (e.g., deserters), on the assumption that they either share the culprits' views or are apt to be guilty of complicity.[21]

In some cases the elimination amounts to purposive prophylaxis initiated by the leadership. In others the segregation or removal is based on an almost paranoid extension of the criteria of "security"—essentially reactive (or, more correctly, overreactive) moves in response to unanticipated developments.[22]

Characteristically, the terror to which Soviet Jews—in particular, selected prominent and publicly active individuals, such as Markish, Mikhoels, or Lozovsky—were subjected in 1949–53 coincided with a stepped-up propaganda campaign against both "rootless cosmopolitans" and "Zionists," and began soon after the establishment of the state of Israel and evidence of sympathy for it on the part of some Soviet Jews.[23] By derivation from the Soviet milieu, the same "anti-Zionist" theme became central in some of the East European purges, notably in the Slánský trial in 1952. Here, as in the "anti-Zionist" campaign in 1967–68 in Poland (in both cases with anti-intellectual overtones), the foreign inspiration apparently fell on fertile soil.

Several social groups became victims of repressive campaigns because of their exposure to experiences outside of Soviet control: prisoners of war returning from enemy captivity, *Ostarbeiter* (eastern workers) herded to Germany from the occupied areas for forced labor and returning home in 1945, even some Soviet partisans who by dint of circumstances found themselves operating more or less autonomously behind enemy lines and

[21] Based on Gliksman, "Social Prophylaxis," pp. 68–69. The expression, "social prophylaxis," appears to have been introduced in this meaning by Beck and Godin, *Russian Purge*, pp. 228–39.

[22] On the removal of the Crimean Tatars, Kalmyks, Balkars, Karachai, Chechens, and Ingushi, see Conquest, *The Soviet Deportation of Nationalities*; and, with some reservations, Institute for the Study of the USSR, *Genocide in the USSR*. On the deportation of ethnic minorities prior to World War II, see, for example, Weissberg, *The Accused*, p. 10. The closest analog to such "security" measures of preventive terror is the treatment of Japanese-Americans during World War II in the United States, and of various tribal groups in the British colonies. Another form of social prophylaxis sanctioned in the West is compulsory preventive confinement in mental institutions.

[23] Probably capitalizing on residual elements of "popular" antisemitism (all the while denying it), the Soviet silencing or removal of prominent individuals served to intimidate the rest of the Jewish community, thus minimizing the risks of what the leadership evidently considered their divided loyalty. See, for example, Gregor Aronson, "The Jewish Question During the Stalin Era," in Aronson et al., eds., *Russian Jewry 1917–1967*; Solomon Schwarz, *Evrei v Sovetskom Soiuze . . . 1939–1965 gg.*

now were suspected of having acquired habits of spontaneity and disregard for authority. These and other groups were subjected to procedures of "filtration," that is, screening and selective segregation, with a wide range of possible verdicts awaiting them. In many instances, their next of kin were made to share the fate of convicts and suspects, too. In Eastern Europe, a number of "Londoners" among Communist cadres were similarly purged in 1949–53. The dependents may have been involved for the sake of sheer intimidation and retribution, but the real targets of the Soviet campaign, more often than not, were not its immediate victims but the rank and file, who, the leadership seemed to believe, needed to be shielded from these carriers of incongruent values.

Soviet practice has thus ranged from the elimination of individuals, to case-by-case review, to random exile or arrest of percentages of specified occupational or socioeconomic groups, to the removal of entire groups. The very range of these activities contributed to a state of diffuse terror in the population. No citizen could be sure that he would not become a suspect. The resulting anxiety may indeed reflect what can only be surmise at this stage, namely, that the selection, sequence, and scope of "target groups" for prophylactic terror in the Stalin days was not the product of a carefully drawn-up master plan but, far more likely, the product of incremental decisions in response to various pressures on the leadership.

Except where there are clear security needs, social prophylaxis applied to *a priori* groups is not a matter of the highest priority, even to Communist regimes. By and large, mechanisms of control must be assumed to operate adequately at the mobilization stage to apprehend active malefactors, to contain and deter even the spread of "dangerous" views and values, and to cut off the population from contact with the outside world. This low priority, in all likelihood, is why Communist systems other than the Soviet have only rarely engaged in such wholesale preemption. Even the East European regimes in their "satellite" days had other, greater, worries and problems, and governments tend to stagger tasks and assign sequential priorities of urgency. The Chinese Communists, too, have not engaged in the wholesale deportation of nationality groups. Whether or not other Communist regimes would have moved to such operations remains a matter of sheer speculation. In fact, of course, developments in Moscow dictated the termination, just as they had spelled the beginning, of what for most of the East European regimes was a frustrated or abortive mobilization stage. The fact of Soviet influence only underscores the specificity of Soviet approaches and techniques; it does not undermine the argument that authentic Communist regimes will strive by other means, perhaps, to contain and isolate incongruent values.

Other Functions

Political terror serves a variety of functions, some welcome and some not in the eyes of those who employ it. The mobilization function of political purges may be assumed to be among the desired functions: by stirring feelings of commitment, loyalty, and patriotism among those who believe its line and against those who are ostensibly, and "admittedly," alien elements or outright traitors; by bringing home the need for eternal vigilance against subversives; and by producing scapegoats to be blamed for the regime's failings, the surviving leadership presumably reaps normative rewards for the expenditure of coercive power.[24]

No less welcome to some are the opportunities for vertical mobility, typically extending through the bureaucracy, since the elimination of elite figures as part of the purge frequently leads to the ouster of their subordinates as well. Political purges thus lead to the advancement of new cadres to fill the vacancies created by the application of terror, an outcome that is functional to the extent that it may replace old revolutionaries with better-trained as well as more pliant and more dependent cadres.

---

[24] See, for example, Tibor Szamuely, "The Elimination of Opposition Between the 16th and 17th Congresses of the CPSU." On other links between coercive and normative effects, see also below, pp. 125–26.

We find no evidence, however, to support the view that such replacement of technically incompetent veterans of the revolution with men of greater and more highly specialized skills, is a central aim of those who initiate the process, whether in the Great Purge in the Soviet Union or in the "anti-Titoist" campaign in Eastern Europe. Objectively, in any event, the circulation of sub-elites does serve to forestall the "crystallization of autonomous islands of countervailing force."[25]

The change in the composition of the Communist party is particularly striking in the Soviet case. As a recent study shows, almost 60 per cent of its membership at the beginning of 1933 were no longer in the party by the beginning of 1939. However, whereas the CPSU had in 1928 included only 1.2 per cent of all "specialists" in the Soviet Union, by 1939 it counted 20.6 per cent of all specialists among its members (and this percentage was now based on a total membership five times as large as a decade earlier).[26] To be sure, such a change might have been accomplished by a simple expansion of party ranks—and a substantial part of the purge and turnover in party membership did not in fact involve terror—yet an important part, especially among leading members, did: one characteristic of the *Yezhovshchina* is precisely that in its course terror and purge "merged into one gigantic operation."[27]

Moreover, a Communist leadership is bound to view all bureaucracies as constraints on its own freedom of action. Stalin used the secret police against the bureaucracy; Khrushchev suffered the consequences of tacit bureaucratic foot-dragging and sabotage; Mao Tse-tung sought to use the Red Guards against

---

[25] Fainsod, *How Russia Is Ruled*, p. 441. It would indeed be stretching the point beyond reason to suggest that the chain reaction begun, say, by the murder of Kirov was *intended* to bring into office a new generation both "red" and "expert." Moreover, even the consequences of the terror are not unambiguous on this score. Many "old Bolsheviks" were purged, but so were many experts, including military commanders and scientists, as well as leaders of the younger generation. "It was plain as early as 1937 that the overwhelming majority of arrested Party officials . . . by no means belonged to the old-guard type, and that liquidation was being applied on a far wider scale." (Beck and Godin, *Russian Purge*, p. 253.)

[26] A. L. Unger, "Stalin's Renewal of the Leading Stratum: A Note on the Great Purge." See also Harry Rigby, *Communist Party Membership in the USSR*, ch. 6.

[27] Brzezinski points this out, in *Permanent Purge*, p. 65.

the bureaucracy as functional surrogates of the NKVD. As a
study of the Chinese bureaucracy points out with reference to
the mid-1960's:

Power and influence still appear to be vested as much in individuals
as in bureaucratic positions. Purging—with public denunciations—
appeared to be almost the only way to destroy the influence of many
ageing leaders. The Great Proletarian Cultural Revolution can also
be seen, therefore, as a response to the persistence of traditionalism.
The purge eliminated officials whom the system did not seem to be
able to eliminate by other means. It also attacked those officials who
gave primacy to the interests of their local communities, persons who
had, in effect, become "local" rather than "outside" leaders.[28]

Thus the elimination, circulation, and galvanization of bureaucracies—usually a secondary outcome of high-level purges
—are typically perceived to be desirable in untying the leader's
hands. They may also be productive of greater efficiency, application, and higher quality of performance.[29]

Political terror may also be viewed as serving certain economic
functions, not only the obvious processes of industrialization
and collectivization of agriculture, which are subsumed under
the mobilization syndrome, but also the employment as forced
labor of large masses of convicts and deportees. The forced
labor function was particularly pronounced in the Soviet Union
but was also observable to a lesser degree in China and Eastern
Europe. To be sure, some monuments to their desperate toil
remain to illustrate the uses of forced labor. There even appear
to have been instances of terror applied specifically in order to
provide manpower replacements at times of labor shortage in
the camps, due in some cases to the physical extermination of
earlier deportees. But on balance, the system of camps (with
their millions of inmates in the Stalin era) in the Soviet Union
and in other Communist systems must be viewed as an economically irrational enterprise. It was marked by inordinately high

---

[28] Michel Oksenberg, "Local Leaders in Rural China, 1962–1965," p. 215. For examples of bureaucratic defiance of orders from the political leadership, see Tang Tsou,
"Revolution, Reintegration, and Crisis in Communist China," in Ho and Tsou, *China
in Crisis*, I, 334.

[29] See also Fainsod, "Bureaucracy and Modernization: The Russian and Soviet Case,"
and Carl Beck, "Bureaucracy and Political Development in Eastern Europe."

mortality, a ludicrous waste of skills, general inefficiency, frequent incompetence, and low productivity, not to speak of the human effects on the survivors.[30] It made sense only as a way to get "something for nothing" (or, more precisely, for relatively little), capitalizing on a pool of labor that would otherwise have been doomed to perish "unproductively."

All the available information indicates that economic development was neither intended to be, nor indeed was, the desired result of the liquidation of political figures—say, of a Nikolai Bukharin or a Rudolf Slánský—or of the exile of the next of kin of political oppositionists. Furthermore, the major terror in the Soviet Union came after the decisive breakthrough in the economy had been achieved. Finally, in the Soviet application of similar terror to foreign Communists and to the personnel of the Communist International, economic considerations simply did not exist.

The machinery of political terror does, of course, lend itself to the pursuit of personal or factional ends. It may provide a welcome cloak for the settling of accounts. A Mátyás Rákosi may use it to rid himself of such a rival leader as László Rajk. Factions within the elite may use it for their own ends. Just as pro-Soviet Communists may in Rumania dispose of non-Muscovite Communists (such as Pătrăscanu), protagonists of a national orientation in a dependent regime may dispose of fellow-leaders subservient to foreign—even Soviet—interests (such as Ana Pauker).[31] The contest between Georgi Malenkov and Andrei Zhdanov and their respective followers provides the most plausible background for some of the terror operations in Russia between 1946 and 1951, including the mysterious

[30] On the economic aspects of Soviet labor camps, see Naum Jasny, "Labor and Output in Soviet Concentration Camps"; and S. Swianiewicz, *Forced Labour and Economic Development.* On the forced labor system as a whole, see David Dallin and Boris Nicolaevsky, *Forced Labor in Soviet Russia;* Beck and Godin, *Russian Purge;* and titles listed in Conquest, *The Great Terror,* pp. 573–74. For a hostile but well-documented report on China, see Commission Internationale Contre le Régime Concentrationnaire, *White Book on Forced Labour and Concentration Camps in the People's Republic of China.*
[31] A variant is the liquidation of factions with different foreign orientations, with the connivance of the leader. Thus, in 1950–51 Kim Il-sung purged both pro-Chinese rivals (such as Mu Chang) and pro-Soviet rivals (such as Ho Ka-i) from the North Korean elite. A similar struggle took place in the Albanian leadership.

purges and executions of the "Leningrad Case." Factional rivalry was apparently one reason for the Chinese crisis that led to the ouster of such stalwarts as Liu Shao-ch'i and Teng Hsiao-p'ing. And the Soviet experience after Stalin's death shows how in the absence of a dominant leader a combination of various civilian and military elements can topple as powerful a figure as Lavrenti Beria and his machine.

An escalation of terror campaigns may also be the result of structural features. The very existence of the secret police or its equivalent as a separate, secretive, almost invisible, agency run by ambitious men typically will encourage the spread of terror. Self-interest invites overcompliance and excesses in denunciations and charges against fellow-citizens, largely out of a sense of insecurity felt by subordinates in and out of the secret police.[32] Finally, the system lacks strong countervailing and restraining pressures or institutional checks against the heightening spiral of arbitrariness and the widening circles of implicated "enemies."

Yet the contention that the process as a whole easily gets "out of hand" can scarcely be accepted without qualification. No doubt, in the Great Purge in the Soviet Union, the scope of terror exceeded what the leaders had planned: Stalin in effect said as much, later. No doubt, the information he received about its true dimensions was, at best, inadequate, and even at the time Soviet officials warned against unwarranted and overzealous denunciations.[33] But even at the hysterical peak of terror activi-

---

[32] This is how a former Czech political prisoner described a major in the secret police whom he came to know in the course of his detention: "He possessed an almost religious conviction that everybody without exception was essentially a heretic and a traitor and that all that was needed was to squeeze him to confess. When on occasion he elaborated on this theme he appeared to divide his fellow citizens into two groups: those who have already been broken by his organization and those who were yet to be arrested. He radiated a philosophical outlook that the world was dominated by policemen, and that the purpose of investigation was to unveil the increasingly unbelievable plots, which would provide the apparatus with a justification for their continued existence and him personally with a higher rank, decorations, and a career." (Vladimir Veselý, in *Reporter* [Prague], 19 [1968], cited in Otto Ulč, "Koestler Revisited," p. 120.)

[33] It is true that in Eastern Europe, especially in 1950–52, the local security services seemed to operate half independently of the party leadership. The revelations about the background of the Slánský trial (Kaplan, "Zamyšlení nad politickými procesy") show that Gottwald was not even fully informed of the investigators' activities that resulted in Slánský's arrest and trial. On the other hand, Rákosi went out of his way to mastermind "his" trials as well as to implicate foreign Communists and to supply names of possible "traitors" to the leadership of less fanatical parties, such as the Polish and Czechoslovak parties.

ties, Stalin retained sufficient authority and control to bring to a halt, with perhaps surprising ease, the powerful forces he had unleashed. And the Chinese Communist leadership has alternated between allowing public security agencies greater autonomy during campaigns, on the one hand, and reinstating institutional checks once excesses became obvious, on the other. Only during the Great Proletarian Cultural Revolution did the virtually total destruction of countervailing institutions make possible the unrestrained brutality of the Red Guards.[34]

It remains true that the precedent of earlier terror makes more likely and conscionable the subsequent resort to terror. There is at work a subjective process, a habit-forming adaptation to violence. And, as Alec Nove suggests with reference to the early 1930's in Russia, the failures and miscalculations set the stage for more campaigns: "Once all this happened, the case for coercion was greatly strengthened . . . as part of the necessities of staying in power and continuing the industrial revolution in an environment grown more hostile as a result of such policies."[35] The use of terror becomes a vicious circle: terror provokes hostility that only terror can repress.

The Role of the Dictator

In considering the unique role of the most important actor, the dictator, in the wielding of power, it is well to differentiate his role from his individual personality. Both explanations that argue a single cause—"all system" or "all personality"—are in our view unsatisfactory.[36]

Insofar as the dictator's systemic role is concerned, at the mobilization stage both organizational and ideological authority are typically integrated in his person. That is, he gains clear hegemony over his associates and rivals for control of the party apparatus and establishes himself as the undisputed interpreter of the faith. Political terror then tends to become a key instru-

---

[34] See *China's Legal and Security Systems.*
[35] Nove, *Economic Rationality,* p. 28.
[36] For an approach that seeks to explain the use of terror in Stalinist Russia in terms of systemic variables, see Alexander Gerschenkron, *Continuity in History,* ch. 11; for an exhaustive treatment stressing, on the contrary, the role of personality rather than systemic factors, see Conquest, *The Great Terror.*

ment in his hands to secure if not a personal monopoly of power
then at least clear de facto predominance. Once having achieved
that, being ever suspicious of his subordinates, and inevitably
isolated from access to objective intelligence, the dictator tends
to act as if *his* security depended on the insecurity of his immediate associates and subordinates. By his behavior he may then
unwittingly engender considerable anxiety in his entourage, or
he may quite consciously seek to play off his associates against
each other, thus maximizing their dependence on his goodwill.
Ultimately "the paranoia produced by the isolation of the leadership also penetrates to the lower levels of the totalitarian
hierarchy."[37]

Although we incline to the view that there is such a structural
tendency toward mutually reinforcing insecurity, we do not
argue that it must manifest itself in every case. Cultural, personal, or accidental factors may intervene to override this built-
in bias. Thus, over and above this general tendency, the personality and style of any particular dictator may be decisive in defining the scope, the virulence, the frequency, the methods—
and the victims—of terror. Surely no adequate explanation of
specific instances of political terror under Stalin could fail to
give full weight to his own part, be it in the purge of Red Army
officers, or in the liquidation of Nikolai Voznesensky, or in the
preparation of the "Doctors' Plot."

It is not necessary for our purposes to decide whether or not
Stalin was in fact suffering from and acting out paranoid de-
lusions.[38] In any case, he was in control of the terror. Obviously
there is nothing in the system as such that would require the
dictator to convert every instance of perceived disagreement

---

[37] Brzezinski, *Permanent Purge*, p. 16. See also Fainsod, *How Russia Is Ruled*, pp.
423–44; Moore, *Terror and Progress*, pp. 13–15; and Conquest, *The Great Terror*, *passim*. "In 1931 a forbidden anecdote went the rounds among Party members in Moscow.
Yagoda, the head of the GPU, was alleged to have asked Stalin: 'Which would you prefer, Comrade Stalin: that Party members should be loyal to you from conviction or
from fear?' And Stalin is alleged to have replied: 'From fear.' Whereupon Yagoda asked,
'Why?' To which Stalin replied: 'Because convictions can change: fear remains.' The
story is in all probability apocryphal; above all, because Stalin had no sense of self-
irony." (Weissberg, *The Accused*, p. 510.)

[38] The case for Stalin's paranoia, presented by more than one author, is well argued
in Tucker, "Introduction," to Tucker and Cohen, eds., *The Great Purge Trial*, which
also rebuts the view of the Great Purge as a functional requisite of the Soviet system,
arguing instead that it reflected "Stalin's own needs, both political and psychological."

into a case of betrayal; or to rationalize his own behavior by imputing to all his enemies—real and imagined, domestic and foreign, "left" and "right"—a common conspiracy; or to insist on liquidations concealed by a panoply of artifacts, such as forced confessions and public show trials, and the pretense of judicial process. Khrushchev's secret speech offers ample confirmation of the view that Stalin did indeed develop a suspiciousness peculiarly his own that had serious effects on the Soviet system. But to say that the system made Stalin possible is not to say that it made him either necessary or inevitable.

It seems more useful to inquire into the interaction of the causal variables—both the effect of the system on the personality of the leader[39] and the effect of his personality on the system.[40] The commitment to drastic, centrally directed change, the general orientation toward totalism, the siege mentality, the insistence on hierarchical organization and discipline, the inevitable intelligence failures in a high-coercion system: these are but a few of the elements bound to reinforce the particular predispositions in Stalin that made more likely his widespread but cunning use of terrror. Some but not all of the same variables were influencing other Communist leaders—Mao, Tito, Castro—who, given their different personalities, responded in different ways. In turn, the effect of the leader's personality may well be seen not only in Soviet bureaucratic style and the "institutionalization of paranoia," but also in other systems. Rákosi, in Hungary, is a case in point.

The extent of brutalization of human sensitivities cannot be explained by the manifest or latent hostility of the Hungarian people to communism. . . . Possibly Rákosi thought that Stalin would be pleased with nothing less. Possibly he gave free reign to his own penchant for violence and inhumaneness, which he had long held in check.[41]

---

[39] Obviously, "behavior . . . is a function of both the environmental situations in which actors find themselves and the psychological predispositions they bring to these situations." (F. I. Greenstein, *Personality and Politics*, p. 7.)

[40] Raymond Aron, *Démocratie et totalitarisme*, pp. 275–302, comes closest to such an "interaction" approach. He points out that what made the personality cult possible were not only the peculiarities of the leader but also the organizational techniques and the action style of the CPSU. In his opinion, the full horror of the 1934–38 period resulted from the confluence of police terror and "ideological frenzy" caused by the total politicization of public life. Hence, whereas the personality of the leader was of consequence, such pathological forms of despotism presupposed ideological frenzy.

[41] Zinner, *Revolution in Hungary*, p. 114.

No doubt the effect of his personality on the system was one—
but only one—of the causes of the revolution in 1956.

Atomization

One characteristic outcome of the application of political terror in Communist systems is the widespread psychological
insulation of individuals, for terror tends to disrupt not only
traditional patterns but also interpersonal bonds. After some
exposure to terror—and evidently even after mere hearsay experience with it—people seem to move to a gradual avoidance
of vulnerabilities, to adopt habits of inhibition and self-isola-
tion, tendencies that became particularly intense at the height of
the Stalin era because of the hazards of meaningful interpersonal
communication. Memoirs and "documentary" fiction abound
in examples of friends, associates, and relatives being abandoned or studiedly ignored by those who feared the possible
consequences of an association with anyone who might some-
how have been implicated as an "enemy of the people."[42] Thus,
the label of "atomization," often applied to totalitarian systems,[43] is generally apt for the mobilization stage. It would appear, however, that atomization is a by-product of terror
(though apparently one entirely welcome to the regime) rather
than the result of conscious policy-making.

The condition of an atomized society is fully congruent with
the objective of totally committing all resources to the goals of
the leadership by destroying all links and bonds, formal and informal, except those that the regime itself creates and manipu-
lates as "transmission belts."[44] Such a society is, after all, but a
special and peculiarly complex case of what have been labeled

[42] For an interesting account of "creeping atomization" in China, see Ezra Vogel,
"From Friendship to Comradeship: The Change in Personal Relations in Communist
China."
[43] Unless otherwise indicated, we use the term "totalitarian" to refer to the mobilization stage of Communist development. For recent contributions to the debate over "totalitarianism," see Johnson, ed., *Change in Communist Systems*, and Friedrich, et al.,
Totalitarianism in Perspective.
[44] See Moore, *Terror and Progress*, pp. 158–59. In our sense, an "atomized" society
goes beyond the generic characteristic of a mass society, in which individuals are "inter-
connected only by virtue of their common ties to [the national state]." (William Kornhauser, *The Politics of Mass Society*, p. 75.)

"total institutions," such as prisons, asylums, and army camps, characterized, among other things, by the prohibition of social intercourse with the outside world and of departure into it. Among the features typical of such institutions—along with the staff function of surveillance, the incidence of confessions, and the numerous actively enforced rulings—is something resembling the mechanism of atomization: "In total institutions staying out of trouble is likely to require persistent conscious effort. The inmate may forego certain levels of sociability with his fellows to avoid possible incidents."[45] In a Communist system, moreover, such atomization minimizes the chances for communication or organization among deviants, thus serving the regime's security interests while making the individual all the more vulnerable to official persuasion and coercion in the absence of viable alternatives.

In the mobilization stage for the particular system we have described, then, atomization is functional. But ultimately rulers even in Communist polities tend to recognize that social disorganization cannot be a foundation for permanence. Not only in utopian-ideological but also in operational terms, reintegration along new lines must remain alive, if only as a postponed objective. The Chinese Communist leadership has remained well aware of this need for a new pattern of roles and expectations; in contrast—and this circumstance deserves further examination—Stalin, for one, behaved as if he had concluded that he did not wish or could not afford to move from atomization and a façade of consensus to reintegration and genuine consent.

[45] Erving Goffman, "On the Character of Total Institutions," in his *Asylums*, p. 43. "Institutions for adult socialization are most effective . . . when they manage to exclude counteracting social stimuli through isolation of the trainees, to maintain consistent goals within the institution, to manipulate rewards and punishments in the service of official training goals. . . . A complete social environment in which the individual becomes temporarily involved may be necessary to effect drastic alterations in his motives, habits, and values after childhood." (Robert LeVine, "Political Socialization and Culture Change," pp. 301–2.)

4 The Mobilization Stage: Two Orientations

Administer a powerful shock to the patient and yell at him,
"You're ill! so that he is frightened and breaks out all over in a
sweat. Then we will get him to take the treatment.

Mao Tse-tung

The contrasting practices of the two prime examples of Communist experience to date can be analyzed in terms of the regimes' different orientations toward the relative importance of middle- and long-range goals. It would be a serious error to see the differences characterizing the Stalinist and Maoist approaches as absolute, if only because the Chinese experience has itself exhibited significant variations over time, but it is appropriate to conceive of the dominant Soviet and Chinese orientations to political control and coercion as tending toward opposite poles.

On the Soviet side, the particular concern with middle-range goals is no doubt rooted both in the political-cultural environment of Russia and Bolshevism and in Stalin's own personality. Along with his extraordinary intolerance, vengefulness, and suspiciousness, Stalin was intensely committed not to brook either autonomy or deviance. At the same time, he was responsible for a peculiar construct of a world of make-believe, stemming perhaps from an inordinate preoccupation with acting out a fictitious drama on the stage of history, a drama that required him to manipulate reality so as to conform with his myths. Though by no means unique, his concern with rewriting history falls into this pattern; so does his insistence on the use of dissimulating labels and institutions, and his elaborate sponsorship of blatantly spurious practices, such as false confessions, contrived amalgams of incompatible conspirators, and the disguising of the forced-labor system.[1]

One consequence of this orientation was Stalin's overriding concern with the façade of individual performance—that is, with compliant behavior. Inkeles and Bauer found it to be generally characteristic of official attitudes that Soviet policy toward loyal citizens was behaviorally indistinguishable from policy toward disloyal ones—fully in line with the sweeping suspiciousness of the master, to whom every citizen was a potential enemy.[2] Thus logically the operational consequence was an attempt to control the entire environment so that the citizen had no choice but to comply.

Rather realistically, then, Stalin's concern was not with the future Communist society but with the here and now. The far-ranging and at one time imaginative discussions about "the new Soviet man" therefore tended under Stalin to become another bit of fiction, an aspect of utopia relevant only to shape and justify everyday practices.[3] As one study suggests,

all values the regime tried to inculcate were instrumental rather than ultimate ones. Simultaneously, it was recognized as dysfunctional for totalitarian regimes to attempt to inculcate ultimate values. Ultimate values of any kind, once internalized, tend to become sources of autonomy and independence for the individual.[4]

Implicit in Stalin's orientation was the assumption that a combination of political socialization, insulation from incongruent values, and coercion (as well as its anticipation) would result in conforming behavior: a sequence of compliances with

---

[1] The fact that this concern was not purely idiosyncratic is illustrated by the Soviet insistence, in 1969, to secure from the Czechoslovak leadership a retroactive endorsement of the Soviet invasion of the previous year.

[2] *The Soviet Citizen*, pp. 282ff.
There is an interesting parallel in the orientation of the Nazi leadership. Thus Joseph Goebbels made "an important distinction . . . between *Stimmung* and *Haltung*. The mood of the people might fluctuate, they might get depressed, but this was of lesser importance as long as . . . their active support of the war effort remained unimpaired." (Ernest Bramsted, *Goebbels and National Socialist Propaganda 1925–1945*, p. 276.)

[3] Stalin's public statements and writings in the mobilization phase are strikingly lacking in discussions of the nature of the future Communist society.

[4] Paul Hollander, "The New Man and His Enemies: A Study of the Stalinist Conceptions of Good and Evil Personified." See also his "Models of Behavior in Stalinist Literature."

specific messages would increasingly reinforce the habit of compliance. Such a formula may be viable but it permits no relaxation of coercion, for the incumbent leader can never be certain
what lurks behind the mask of conformity. (It is this stress on
outward behavior that makes possible the survival of what are
at times colloquially labeled as "radishes"—citizens "red on the
outside and white on the inside.") Furthermore, as we shall try
to show, in the long run such a policy of permanent coercion
tends to be viewed as excessively costly and inefficient. Here,
then, is another source of tension, for the necessity of keeping
up the use of coercive power clashes with the desideratum of
moving to a relaxation of coercion for the sake of maximizing
normative and material power.

The most clearcut alternative to this Stalinist approach within the Communist spectrum is to be found in Mao's concern
with the internalization of the value system as an essential middle-range goal. There is here also a definite belief that the formation of a "new man," and of a system based largely on normative
power, must remain a real and vital long-range goal. Indeed, in
doctrine and practice, this goal has been at the base of such
profound attempts to transform the individual as thought reform campaigns and the Great Proletarian Cultural Revolution.
The Maoist formula thus stresses the change in underlying attitudes to be brought about by internalization of the desired value
structure, through a very different mix of coercion and persuasion—a far more ambitious, difficult, and distant aim than the
Stalinist.

By definition, then, the Soviet orientation permitted and indeed even required far greater stress on coercive power; moreover, the resort to the use of coercion was rationalized by theories
contrived to "prove" the increasing need for coercion.

The distinction between the control of behavior on the one
hand and the control of attitudes on the other may be thought
of as polar positions on a spectrum ranging from minimal to
maximal objectives (a characteristic Leninist approach). This
conception, moreover, helps to explain why one orientation—
Stalin's—is content to see as its target societal "atomization"

(the disruption of traditional patterns and insulation from incongruent values), whereas the other—Mao's—aims at a reintegration of the individual into a new value structure.

Thought Reform

In both theory and practice, the Chinese approach to political terror reveals significant distinctive features. The use of terror, as a manifest, purposive transaction in the service of the government or the ruling party, has been far more restricted in China than it had been at a comparable stage in Soviet Russia or Eastern Europe. Likewise, the Public Security Bureau in China has not enjoyed the power or autonomy of the NKVD (or its successor agencies up to 1953); China has seen no prophylactic liquidations of entire social groups and—at least until the Cultural Revolution—no witchhunts to destroy subordinate bureaucracies of purged officials.

The general proclivity of the Chinese leadership to give relatively greater weight to normative power in the mix of sanction systems appears to be rooted in the Confucian emphasis on learning, contemplation, and self-analysis, which, we are told, has left an imprint on the values of the Communist elite; in Confucius' words, "the cultivation of the person depends upon rectifying the mind."[5] It is true that other elements of the same tradition—incongruent with Maoist values—have been vigorously rejected in China, the outstanding example being Confucianism's separation of mental and manual labor. Communist receptivity to this particular aspect of Confucian tradition must then be explained, for in doctrine Chinese Communism—like its Soviet and East European counterparts—sanctions violence not only in the pursuit but also in the exercise of power.[6] There

[5] See, for example, Ping-ti Ho, "Salient Aspects of China's Heritage," in Ho and Tsou, *China in Crisis*, I, 32. Frederick T.C. Yu also refers to Mencius' saying "When men are subdued by force, they do not submit in their hearts," in his *Mass Persuasion in China*, p. 39.

[6] Both before and under Mao, the party affirmed the use of "violence and terror as a means of revolutionary agitation" (to use Stuart Schram's words). Numerous statements of the leadership could be adduced to support this view, even though they are often accompanied by admonitions to rely first and foremost on techniques of socialization. See Schram, *Mao Tse-tung*, pp. 110–11, 119–20, 238; *Communist China 1955–1959: Policy Documents with Analysis, passim*; Arthur Gundersheim, "Terror and Political Control in Communist China" (permission of the Center for Social Organization

is, moreover, no question about the supremacy of politics and the political leadership over economics and law. And the Chinese leadership has repeatedly reaffirmed its concern with the "handling of contradictions" within the system, with an emphasis on volition, "consciousness" and "re-education."

It is apparent that the experience of the civil war years was decisive in shaping these attitudes of the Maoist elite. Among the features of the "Yenan complex" is a stress on pragmatism in techniques; a reliance in practice on small groups (that inevitably were somewhat autonomous) as units of discussion, interaction, and decision-making; and an emphasis on gaining popular goodwill and engaging in political education—all virtual necessities under conditions of guerrilla warfare.[7] As a result, Chinese Communism has stressed, both in doctrine and in practical directives, "voluntarism" and "activism" to a degree incompatible with the Stalinist approach.[8]

The civil war years in China likewise provided a laboratory for techniques of public self-criticism and confession, leading among other things to the conviction that even class enemies need not be exterminated but may be successfully "re-educated." As one authoritative commentary suggests, "Instead of deducing ideological tendencies from class affiliations, [the Chinese Communists decided] to deduce class affiliations from ideological tendencies."[9] While recognizing that "certain diehard counter-

Studies, University of Chicago to cite this manuscript is gratefully acknowledged); Frame, "Dialectical Historicism"; Schein, *Coercive Persuasion*; and Lifton, *Thought Reform and the Psychology of Totalism*. For documents showing a decision of the Chinese leadership to handle the rectification of abuses leniently in the period between the Great Leap and the Cultural Revolution, see C. S. Chen, ed., *Rural People's Communes in Lien-chiang . . . 1962–1963*, pp. 47, 167–68.

[7] See Chalmers Johnson, "Building a Communist Nation in China," and his "Chinese Communist Leadership and Mass Response: The Yenan Period and the Socialist Education Campaign Period," pp. 397ff, and Kenneth Lieberthal, "Tactics, Goals and Social Composition: Differences Between the Soviet and Chinese Communist Parties." Former Politburo member Chang Kuo-t'ao traces the origin of the *hsueh-hsi* (literally, "self-study") tradition to the experience of the guerrilla army. (Barnett, *Communist China: The Early Years*, p. 102; and Lifton, *Thought Reform*, pp. 393–95.) On the specific role of the "small group" in China, see Franz Schurmann, "Organization and Response in Communist China."

[8] See Vogel, "Voluntarism and Social Control," pp. 168–84. See also Schein, *Coercive Persuasion*.

[9] Conrad Brandt, John Fairbank, and Benjamin Schwartz, eds., *A Documentary History of Chinese Communism*, p. 320. The redemption of class enemies is often invoked with the formula, "Cure the disease, save the man." As Richard Lowenthal observes, "The

revolutionaries will be suppressed," Mao and his associates have emphasized that at least under Chinese conditions former land-owners and members of the urban bourgeoisie can be transformed into useful members of society. It is this outlook that has found expression in the peculiarly Chinese amalgam of terror and persuasion known as "thought reform," which reflects precisely the orientation outlined above, namely, the need to change not only behavior but also underlying attitudes and beliefs.[10]

Thought reform is thus one Chinese answer to the universal Communist problem of mobilizing normative assets and also to the more specific problem of insulating certain strata of the population from incongruent values. The coercive element in thought reform, in addition to its widespread but by no means exclusive application in prison situations, includes a form of therapeutic terror. This is indeed how Mao Tse-tung saw it in his "Oppose the Party 'Eight-Legged Essay' " in 1942, in which he viewed the citizen as a patient in need of treatment.[11] The treatment he prescribed included an elaborate process of repudiating the past and severing emotional ties with it, public confession, and exposure to constant small-group interaction during which social pressure to implement a thorough inculcation of official values was applied. The central objective, then, is the reshaping of attitudes, with the small group being the focal milieu and the line between persuasion and compulsion being a fine one indeed.

Thought reform has been the comprehensive label for a variety of activities that have been aptly though paradoxically labeled "coercive persuasion." There is little doubt that the formal appeal to voluntarism does in fact typically involve threats, intimidation, and pressures that produce terror in the

term 'liquidation of classes' is not to be found in Mao's political dictionary. According to his theory, it is only the old class situation that is liquidated—the function, but not necessarily the persons." (*World Communism*, p. 113.)

[10] It should be noted that thought reform was also attempted in North Korea, though on a lesser scale than in China. It is not clear whether this was a mere copying of Chinese techniques.

[11] Mao Tse-tung, "Oppose the Party 'Eight-Legged Essay' " (Feb. 8, 1942); cited in Arthur Cohen, *The Communism of Mao Tse-tung*, p. 197.

form of intense personal anxiety. But except for some inmates of Chinese jails and special categories of recalcitrants the process does not appear to call for any physical violence.

Thought reform may involve almost no coercion or a great deal, for its processes range from genuine "self-study," for example, through public censure requiring repentance and "speak–reason–struggle" sessions, to harassment by activist cadres, mobs, or fellow-members of small groups, along with threats of status loss and material deprivation. Typically the thought reform experience is prolonged. Unlike their Soviet and East European counterparts, the Chinese Communists have looked upon a prisoner's confession as a means, rather than an end in itself. Even in dealing with "counterrevolutionaries," physical violence appears normally to have been avoided for extracting confessions. And once the victim had confessed, he began a long process of re-evaluating his assumptions and "reforming" his thoughts.[12]

There was also a high degree of demonstration terror, with public accusations and required self-criticism that were directed, in the early years, against landlords and "counterrevolutionaries" and, later on, against bureaucrats, businessmen, and intellectuals. One refugee reported:

Especially everyone is afraid of the big meetings where there are 1,000 and 2,000 people, all there to criticize one person. This target of criticism will be in the middle of the group and everyone will shout at him, and the meeting will go on for three or four hours at a time, and there may be several such meetings as this, and very often the person who is criticized will be crying or will be trembling.[13]

But the most widespread and typical forum for thought reform is the small group. "One aim of the discussion process is to have aired all possible heterodox views and then to have the group demolish them through criticism and self-criticism. ... No one can be a passive participant in such a group, and

[12] For an autobiographical account of the thought-reform process in a prison for "counterrevolutionaries" that stresses the persuasiveness of moral argument under conditions of "forced choice" rather than purposive physical violence, see Allyn and Adele Rickett, *Prisoners of Liberation.*
[13] Vogel, unpublished interview, cited in Gundersheim, pp. 83–84.

discussion on a question is not ended until each member expresses acceptance of the 'correct' Party line."[14] Perhaps the most striking aspect of the whole process is the intense social pressure marshaled against the "offender."

In a sense, every member of a *hsueh hsi* group is a minority of one being worked on by all the rest. Some of the groups are composed of people who may be skeptical of the Communist line, yet in these groups a remarkable phenomenon occurs: eight or ten skeptics all exert pressure on each other to become believers—under the watchful eye of the group leader.[15]

The typical process involves a sophisticated assault on the individual's identity (to use Lifton's term), requiring a confession of past sins, not only of specific acts but also of underlying "bourgeois" or other inimical, antisocial, irresponsible, selfish, or deviationist attitudes and beliefs. The sustained group discussion of these "crimes" leads to an "unfreezing" of the individual's perceptions, assumptions, and attitudes regarding his character and his relations with others. This, in turn, is expected to lead to a willing, even eager, acceptance of a new, socially approved moral doctrine and new personal and social values that are then, at least in theory, "refrozen," with appropriate sanctions and incentives being provided at every step.[16]

One study of thought reform has pointed out that the Chinese

---

[14] Barnett, *Communist China*, p. 50. See also Vogel, "Voluntarism and Social Control"; and Jerome Cohen, "The Criminal Process in China."

[15] Barnett, *Communist China*, p. 96.

[16] The most comprehensive and stimulating discussions are in Schein, *Coercive Persuasion*, and Lifton, *Thought Reform*. Lifton (pp. 66–80) describes and analyzes in detail the characteristic phases of the process (at least in an extreme prison setting, which provides a more "ideal" opportunity for control of the total environment). He compares the process of thought reform to "an agonizing drama of death and rebirth": the environment "brings to bear upon the prisoner a series of overwhelming pressures, at the same time allowing only a very limited set of alternatives for adapting to them. In the interplay between person and environment, a sequence of steps . . . revolve around two policies and two demands: the fluctuation between assault and leniency, and the requirements of confession and reeducation. . . . Death and rebirth, even when symbolic, affect one's entire being, but especially that part related to loyalties and beliefs . . . to one's sense of inner identity." As pressure is applied, "Some degree of self-betrayal is quickly seen as a way to survival." The loss of identity is carefully nurtured until the individual loses his capacity to cope with his environment, a state in which he fears annihilation and from which he desperately seeks relief. When then the official attitude suddenly shifts to leniency, he is ready to accept as part of himself "the two basic identities of thought reform": that of the repentant sinner and that of the receptive criminal, who not only concurs "in the environment's legal and moral judgment of him, but also [commits] himself to acquiring the beliefs, values, and identities officially considered desirable."

approach differs from the Soviet practice in the following ways, among others: it seeks to bring about lasting attitude changes and to establish a new moral code; it makes intensive use of group interaction; rather than being limited to party members (as in the Soviet Union), "the ritual of public self-criticism, confession, self-degradation, punishment, and rehabilitation" has been extended to reform even "enemies of the people"; and "a confession is only a prelude to a long period of indoctrination and re-education, which may go on for years and is not terminated until the authorities believe that [the subject] has finally adopted the 'correct' attitude and behavior."[17]

How successful is thought reform? Even the participants, we are told, are uncertain of the results. One analyst reports that among those who have experienced it one may distinguish "the obviously confused, the apparent converts, and the apparent resisters."[18] Some eyewitnesses and specialists—political scientists and psychologists who have interviewed refugees in Hong Kong—have been impressed by the apparent successes scored by the Chinese in remolding beliefs and attitudes at least for the short run. The individual's helplessness and the social pressure to which he is exposed, another writer observes, make resistance ineffective and undesirable.[19] Indeed, it is evidently true that the pressure accomplishes its purpose, and so does the con-

---

[17] Paraphrased from Lawrence Hinkle and H.G. Wolff, "Communist Interrogation and Indoctrination of 'Enemies of the State' " (1956), cited in Arthur Cohen, *The Communism of Mao Tse-tung*, p. 131.

[18] Lifton, *Thought Reform*, pp. 86–87; see also pp. 227–28, 270.

[19] Vogel, "Voluntarism and Social Control," p. 184. One perceptive analyst has summarized her own experience in the process in these terms: "What are the factors which tend to make group study, tense and painful as it often is, effective? First, there is the essential human need to belong, to achieve and maintain emotional balance. To be unprogressive in China is not simply a political verdict; it is social suicide as well. Second, the constant repetition of correct ideas and particularly the application of them to the public analysis of one's own and others' problems mean that one is forced to give them detailed scrutiny. The Communists are conscious of the value of this. 'From habit or pretense,' they say, 'it may become real.' Third—and this is all too often neglected by outside observers—is the crusading idealism, the strong moral note, that runs through all discussion of political, social, and economic steps.... Fourth, there is the universal knowledge, as the highest spokesmen of the Party have frankly admitted, that in the long run no course but the correct one is open. Attempts to avoid the tensions of group study by tacit compact to go through the routine or to stick to pleasantries are blocked not only by the fact of the [group] leader's relations with the authorities but by the ever-present possibility that some member, whether motivated by genuine change of heart or by a selfish attempt at winning official favor, might report the group. Thus, there is tremendous pressure both to fall in line and to want to fall in line." (Harriet Mills, "Thought Reform: Ideological Remolding in China," p. 73.)

trast between earnestness and severity on the one hand and leniency after confession and "unfreezing" on the other. As for the person's frame of mind after he has undergone thought reform, there are indications that it alienates the individual less than did Soviet-style terror.

On balance, however, it is clear that the use of thought reform cannot succeed in creating "a new man in a new society." It evidently generates widespread distrust and tension in interpersonal relations, as well as more general psychological strain and disorder. Even those who "successfully" complete the experience often come away with new doubts and repressed conflicts.[20] But ironically—in light of the difference between Chinese and Soviet orientations—the Chinese practice also appears typically to result in surface compliance.

One may assume that the Chinese leadership itself recognized the failure of its most ambitious goals. As the focus of its efforts shifted in the 1960's to new priorities, thought reform was permitted to wither. The Chinese leadership on this as on other occasions had overreached itself, although the political-ideological and moral orientations underlying the attempt seem to continue to influence its policy and behavior.

Meanwhile, even in China political terror of the physically violent variety has not been entirely eschewed. It was used after the takeover to consolidate political control, to mobilize the population, and to neutralize parts of the prerevolutionary elite. Even then, it is true, the victims were often held up as "educational" examples. Mao admitted in February 1957 that in the first five years of Communist rule some 800,000 "enemies of the people" had been killed. Others have estimated the total number of victims to be somewhere between one and three million— i.e., possibly one-third or one-half of 1 per cent of the population.[21] Yet unquestionably the total amount of purposive terror

[20] See Barnett, *Communist China*, pp. 99–102; Lifton, *Thought Reform*, pp. 398ff; Schein, *Coercive Persuasion*, pp. 157–66. Lifton's interesting theory of psychocultural factors, such as filial piety, cannot be examined here.

[21] See, for example, Gundersheim, "Terror and Political Control in Communist China," p. 2.

initiated by the Communist Chinese regime has been propor-
tionately well below the Soviet level.[22]

Either quantitative or impressionistic cross-cultural compari-
sons may be very misleading here, however. There is reason to
think that individuals in different societies have different
thresholds of "coercion tolerance," that is, they respond with a
different degree of alienation to the same amount of coercion.[23]
Given the highly integrated social structure of the traditional
Chinese village, and the Chinese sensitivity to loss of face or
public shaming, for example, it may take considerably less pressure in China than in Eastern Europe to disrupt the sense of
stability of the mass of the rural population and to induce something akin to terror. (Obviously, variations in personality types
must also be considered.) Thus the amount of coercive power
needed to attain comparable results may be significantly lower
in China than in the Soviet Union or in the West; or, to put it
differently, whereas in China the total of transactions of terror
may be considerably smaller, the output of terror may or may
not be.[24]

One significant variable affecting the ability of the Chinese
leadership to minimize the direct use of terror has been its willingness to go relatively slowly with the particular programs that
have invited intensive terror elsewhere. Indeed, the extreme
phases of rapid mobilization in China are the exceptions that
confirm this rule for it is at those times that the use of terror has
been stepped up. The Cultural Revolution is but the latest case
of such mobilization efforts.

[22] Charles Hoffmann, *Work Incentive Practices and Policies in the People's Republic of China, 1953–1965,* shows the growth of an elaborate system of material incentives for the stimulation of greater productivity. It does not negate the Chinese leadership's concern with attitude modification as a political control mechanism.

[23] See Etzioni, *A Comparative Analysis of Complex Organizations,* p. 312.

[24] It is obvious that the magnitude of the deterrent effect need, at any rate, not vary in proportion to the number of victims. (See, for example, Barnett, *Communist China,* pp. 46–47.)

5 The Mobilization Stage: Transformation Functions

Saboteurs disguise themselves by overfulfilling the plan.
Stalin

The fate of a man was not like a game of chess but like a lottery.
Ilya Ehrenburg

Communist systems are distinguished from other mobilization regimes, among other things, by their leaders' commitment to a utopian vision; and the attempt to move toward its realization requires fundamental transformations in the socioeconomic structure of society, in institutions, in interpersonal relations, and in the very nature of man. Given the high degree of centralized control that a mobilization regime exercises over human and natural resources, it is able, at a price, to embark on directed change toward the attainment of middle-range goals (whether pragmatically or ideologically identified, or both) far more confidently than a less disciplined and less mobilized system.[1] Inevitably, such transformations exact a price and generate hostility, resistance, or alienation, since they are bound to involve a clash with the values, mores, or vested interests of at least some groups. An extra investment of normative or coercive assets is thus required to overcome the friction generated in the course of such a transformation drive; and typically the faster the forward motion, the greater the need for additional coercive power, everything else being equal.

The Cultural Revolution

The socialist transformation of the countryside is the only major process of directed fundamental change that is ideologi-

[1] See the contributions by Johnson and Lowenthal in Johnson, ed., *Change in Communist Systems*. To say that a practical policy is motivated by a utopian vision does not preclude, of course, a more or less rational approach to the selection of the timing, scope, and methods of transformation.

cally required for all Communist polities and in varying degrees has been attempted by all. Only one other major effort at rapid and radical transformation has been made: the Great Proletarian Cultural Revolution of 1966–68 in China.

The traditional Marxist approach had implied that structural changes, such as the nationalization of the means of production, of distribution, and of exchange, and the abolition of the state, would eliminate all causes of human conflict and therefore ultimately would bring about the anticipated transformation in the nature of man. Without explicitly disavowing this expectation, Communist elites elsewhere have tended to adjust to the reality that belied such an orderly and automatic chain reaction. But in China, with Mao's utopian vision essentially intact, the Cultural Revolution was ostensibly intended to make possible precisely such a fundamental transformation. This objective, to be sure, was scarcely in evidence as the struggle among factions, institutions, cliques, and political orientations subjected China to widespread upheaval and violence for some two years.

We are not here concerned with the various interpretations of the events or with the more immediate political objectives of the Chinese leadership.[2] It is too early to assess fully the role of terror in the Cultural Revolution, but there clearly was considerable terror, used in a fashion out of keeping with the accepted "political culture" of Communist China. A good deal of the violence and intimidation, it is true, appears not to have been centrally planned or sanctioned: the whole process was punctuated by autonomous action by Red Guards, army units,

[2] Among the many approaches to an understanding of the Cultural Revolution, Robert Jay Lifton lists "China's (and especially Mao's) 'Yenan Syndrome' or 'Complex,' the nostalgia for the heroic revolutionary methods and achievements of days gone by; China's abrupt loss of a comfortable relationship to her own cultural past; her sense of mounting threat from the outside, especially from America's intervention in Vietnam; and her undergoing a kind of 'Protestant-Catholic dispute' between evangelical reawakening and established bureaucratic compromise." (*Revolutionary Immortality: Mao Tse-tung and the Chinese Cultural Revolution*, p. 6.) The Lifton volume is itself an interesting contribution to the interpretation of the cultural revolution, stressing as it does the inordinate reliance on willpower to achieve fundamental changes. For various significant interpretations, see Franz Schurmann, *Ideology and Organization in Communist China*; Tang Tsou, "Revolution, Reintegration, and Crisis in Communist China," in Ho and Tsou; Philip Bridgham, "Mao's 'Cultural Revolution': Origin and Development"; and Charles Neuhauser, "The Chinese Communist Party in the 1960's: Prelude to the Cultural Revolution."

and "revolutionary rebel committees." This provoked counter-terror by anti-Maoist forces, and virtual civil war in certain regions of the country. One result was a very substantial purge of the Chinese leadership as well as a significant turnover in senior officialdom, with the inevitable consequence that a great deal of vertical mobility became possible.

In this regard, as in some others, there are interesting parallels between the Cultural Revolution and Stalin's Great Purge. But in general the contrast with the Great Purge can be seen in terms of the differences suggested in our earlier discussion of Soviet and Chinese approaches to coercion and directed change. In the words of one analyst,

few victims of the recent Chinese purge suffered physical liquidation or were sent to concentration camps—or indeed were even arrested. The suffering inflicted on the Chinese purge victims has generally been more psychological than physical. Almost all of them were subjected to a harsh ordeal of public "self-criticism" and "struggle" meetings; they were abused and humiliated ... and not a few of them were "tried" by self-appointed kangaroo courts and paraded through the streets with dunce caps on.

Moreover, many of the Chinese purge victims, unlike their Soviet counterparts, "have remained in the public eye ... as targets of contained denunciation in the propaganda media and at mass rallies."[3]

Although the survival of the terrorized victims leaves open the possibility of rehabilitation (and not just posthumous, either), the consequences for the system are not necessarily benign. As has been observed,

it is perhaps because of the Chinese Communists' strong faith in the efficacy of re-education and thought reform that they have rarely resorted to the physical liquidation of those accused of ideological deviation. But it may well prove that this political tradition will hamper and prolong the task of reconsolidation in the wake of the Cultural Revolution.[4]

If its short-term purposes were to combat bureaucratism, "economism," and elite factionalism, the Cultural Revolution

[3] Parris Chang, "Mao's Great Purge: A Political Balance Sheet," p. 9.
[4] *Ibid.*

seems to have exacted an exceedingly high price. It substantially set back the Chinese economy, seriously undermined the regime's support, and virtually destroyed the Communist party's control of the government and of the country. Apparently the utopian commitment to fundamental attitude change was in large measure responsible for letting the leadership set its sights at unrealistic targets and hence turned out to be counterproductive in the end. In any case, the Cultural Revolution remains an exceptional phenomenon among the "transformation" campaigns of the Communist world.

Disintegration and Reintegration in the Countryside

The thrust of Communist "revolutions from above" has been toward the reordering of socioeconomic relations. The development of industry, however, does not require such a fundamental restructuring: factory relationships—such as worker and machine, worker and worker, worker and foreman, management and labor—remain structurally unaltered, whether the owner is an individual, a corporation, or the state. But agriculture is the primary object of centrally directed transformation under Communist regimes. Both the political and the economic control of the countryside rank high among the goals of a Communist regime; likewise, the maximization of agricultural production and procurement and the freeing of rural surplus labor for industry are priority objectives of all Communist regimes committed to economic development and the satisfaction of consumer demands. Thus the collectivization of agriculture and the concomitant political control of the countryside are axiomatic goals in all Communist polities; yet the processes of attaining them vary significantly in ways and means and in the strains and stresses associated with measures of coercion.

Our distinction between the takeover and mobilization stages, it should be remembered, refers only to the dominant processes within these time periods. Hence, mobilization processes may already be evident in the takeover stage. As we have seen, the consolidation of power by Communist regimes typically in-

cludes an attempt to eliminate or neutralize competing authorities, including certain strata of the rural population. Thus in
China, in Russia, and in Eastern Europe, "feudal" elements
were consciously attacked, neutralized, or disposed of soon after
the assumption of power. Furthermore, even before the completion of takeover or power consolidation, such early policies
as the Soviet encouragement of spontaneous land seizure in
1917–18, the forcible expropriation and redistribution of former German lands in Czechoslovakia after World War II, and
controlled land reform in conquered Chinese territory were
only the first phases in agrarian transformation processes that
involved the use of terror.

Our task here is to explore the alternative means used for
pursuing the characteristic goals of Communist regimes vis-à-vis
the agricultural sector, the reasons for their use, and the consequences of such choices. One may assume that a Communist
regime typically seeks to carry out a revolutionary breakthrough
in reordering the patterns of rural stratification and organization. First it attempts to break down existing norms, roles, relations, and expectations; then it tries to reintegrate the peasantry into Communist-controlled structures. These structures
are intended to assure control over the rural population as well
as agricultural produce. Ideological tenets tend to make such a
transformation imperative, but they also circumscribe the range
of what is possible.

True, Poland and Yugoslavia, unwilling or unable to incur
the costs associated with the breakthrough, have indefinitely
postponed or abandoned this process. By failing to destroy the
forces of private property and traditional village organization,
they have made unlikely the adoption of collective structures
and the exploitation of agriculture by the state without violence. In other Communist countries, however, a period of
violent disintegration of the forces of traditionalism has generally been succeeded by the gradual integration of the peasantry into collective or state farms and cooperatives.

The degree and the kind of terror employed in the socialist

transformation of the countryside appear to be largely conditioned by (1) the scope and (2) the speed of the processes employed; (3) the availability of alternative (i.e. normative or utilitarian) sanctions; (4) the unintended consequences of such actions, notably the extent and forms of resistance generated in the process; (5) variations in objective conditions, including the social structure of the peasantry; (6) the level of organizational development, which we take to denote the extent and quality of Communist administrative penetration, the skills of cadres, the reliability and clarity of information, and the degree of lower-level discipline; (7) the synchronization of phases of transformation, meaning the extent to which the processes of disintegration, reintegration, and exploitation are compressed or carried out simultaneously; and (8) elite values, such as the conscious desire of non-Soviet leaders to avoid the high costs and violent aspects of the Soviet experience with collectivization, and the elite's perception of the constraints imposed on the scope of tolerable disruption by such factors as the subsistence level of the population at large. Because the impact of the first five of these variables is self-evident, the following discussion will deal with the last three.

The Chinese Communists sought to destroy pre-Communist rural authorities by employing controlled class warfare, stimulating the poor and middle peasants to unite in class hatred against the rich peasants, and "liquidating the landlords as a class." Although perhaps "only" one-half of 1 per cent of the old landowners were physically eliminated in China during the regime's early years, an authority vacuum, which the Communist party filled, was nevertheless created. Furthermore, the demonstration effect of this terror caused many landlords to flee or recant, and it further emboldened the tradition-bound peasants to take action against their former masters. Apparently this was a consciously manipulated process: "In many villages, land redistribution could have been carried out without violence, but this was not allowed. Class warfare was essential, even though it disrupted agricultural production for long periods of time, because the landlord class had to be discredited thoroughly as well as economically eliminated."[5] Simultaneously, the People's Liberation Army conducted an "anti–local-bully" campaign, terrorizing local gangs and secret societies into submission and dissolution and using selective public trials and executions for demonstration effect. The resulting disintegration of virtually all autonomous and organized rural forces greatly facilitated the further pervasive administrative penetration of the countryside by the Communist party apparatus.

In the Soviet Union, in contrast, opposition to agrarian transformation, symbolized by and attributed to the kulak, since no former landowners were left, was quelled neither by class warfare nor by the demonstration effect of selective public elimination. Rather, between six and ten million kulaks and others ascribed to this ill-defined group were "liquidated as a class"; in most cases they were deported or shot by urban-based cadres who were brought into the rural areas because of the numerical and qualitative inadequacy of Communist cadres there. The failure to incite an active "class struggle" among different strata of the peasantry, on which Soviet planners had counted, derived partly from the lack of a strong rural administrative organization and partly from faulty perception and miscalculation on the part of the decision-makers. The widespread, brutal, and undisciplined use of violence, mostly by "outsiders," in the process of "liquidating" the kulaks and forcing the remaining peasantry into collectives united most of the peasants against the intruding "exploiters." In all likelihood internal class tensions among the peasants had been exaggerated in the first place. To the surprise of Soviet authorities poor and middle peasants showed considerable solidarity, "a strong consciousness . . . as a persecuted social and political class."[6]

[5] Barnett, *Communist China: The Early Years*, p. 271. The Communist leadership was able to learn from its earlier experience by trial and error. Thus Mao later admitted that too much terror had been used during the Kiangsi Soviet period. In particular, Gundersheim ("Terror and Political Control," p. 27) points out that it alienated the middle peasants, who as prime victims of warlords and tax collectors were potential supporters of the revolution.

[6] Ghiţa Ionescu, *The Politics of the European Communist States*, p. 143. It is interesting to note that the same was apparently true in Eastern Europe in the late 1940's.

Communist Eastern Europe was obliged to follow the Soviet model once collectivization was proclaimed to be an immediate and essential objective at the June 1948 session of the Communist Information Bureau. In practice, differences did develop from country to country. Bulgaria, Hungary, and Rumania were the scenes of urban-based assaults on the kulaks, similar in many respects to the Soviet practice a generation earlier but distinctly less extreme. Even so, violence bred violence, and pitched battles were not infrequent. However, unlike the Soviet leadership, the East European regimes for the time being proved more willing and able to settle for partial rather than total elimination of entrenched rural opposition, with transitional forms of cooperatives and private property remaining temporarily predominant, and with the national elites acutely eager to avoid a repetition of the Soviet slaughter and its disastrous consequences.[7]

During the subsequent phase of reintegration, large-scale diffuse violence is not normally required. The destruction of entrenched authorities entails breaking through "systemic opposition" of entire strata whose existence is incompatible with Communist control and transformation, but reintegration and economic exploitation demand coercion only in specific instances of noncompliance with stated policies. Moreover, the demonstration effect of diffuse violence during the phase of revolutionary breakthrough usually carries over into the following period, reducing political opposition to tacit, inchoate, or passive resistance. Middle peasants opposed to cooperativization in China, for instance, are said to have rarely expressed their oppo-

"Attempts to incite class conflict also proved unsuccessful and actually strengthened the opposition," one student concludes. (Andrzej Korbonski, "The Agricultural Problem in East-Central Europe," p. 82.) In Poland, another writes, "even among those peasants who belonged to the Party, the majority were unwilling to join the collectives" (Brzezinski, *Soviet Bloc*, p. 99).

On Soviet collectivization, see Moshe Lewin, *Russian Peasants and Soviet Power*; Nove, *Economic Rationality and Soviet Politics*; Fainsod, *Smolensk*, ch. 12; David Mitrany, *Marx Against the Peasant*; Olga Narkiewicz, "Stalin, War Communism and Collectivization"; and Herbert Ellison, "The Decision to Collectivize Agriculture."

[7] On Eastern Europe, see, for example, Brzezinski, *The Soviet Bloc*; Ionescu, *The Politics of the European Communist States*, pp. 138–45; Lubomir Dellin, "Agriculture and the Peasant"; Korbonski, "The Agricultural Problem in East Central Europe."

sition, having been relegated to a state of "resigned inevitability" during the period of land reform and the campaign against "counterrevolutionaries."[8] Although they had not been the victims in these campaigns, these peasants had evidently become compliant as a result of their perception of the severity of previous coercion and the regime's arbitrary definition of the internal enemy.

Whereas reintegration essentially involving organizational changes within the system typically requires less arbitrary and less severe coercion to secure compliance than does disintegration, the use of terror in this phase again varies among Communist systems. In China the process of cooperativization, which lasted from 1952 to 1957, was relatively nonviolent, proceeding through various phases of "mutual aid teams" and lower- and higher-level cooperatives, with an emphasis on gradualism. A groundwork of administrative penetration and experimentation, capitalizing on the experience accumulated during the civil war, made it possible to resort to such indirect forms of coercion as public criticism and veiled threats, coupled with persuasion, promises of gain, and the manipulation of peasant group interests.[9] Impossible to measure but no doubt an important variable is the distinctive outlook of the Chinese Communists toward the peasantry—part and parcel of the "Yenan syndrome," which we have already mentioned.

In the Soviet Union, however, Stalin was committed to the rapid and simultaneous destruction of traditional authority (i.e. "dekulakization"), reintegration of the peasantry into one dominant type of organization (the kolkhoz), and economic exploitation through forced and at times impossible deliveries of produce to the state. Soviet action thus combined diffuse violence with direct coercion on a massive scale. The rejection of

[8] Thomas Bernstein, "Leadership and Mass Mobilization in the Soviet and Chinese Collectivization Campaigns of 1929–30 and 1955–56: A Comparison," p. 45. We wish to acknowledge our indebtedness to Professor Bernstein for some of the following insights into the role of leadership and bureaucracy in Soviet and Chinese agrarian transformation. See also the stimulating and highly original application of the Etzioni typology in G. W. Skinner and Edwin Winckler, "Compliance Succession in Rural Communist China: A Cyclical Theory."

[9] Bernstein, "Leadership and Mass Mobilization," p. 9.

a gradual transition through intermediate organizational forms, and the weakness of administrative penetration into rural areas made compliance without coercion far more difficult to secure; coercion, in turn, united the peasantry in its resistance. An additional obstacle that was present in Russia but not in China, was the fact that collectivization came on the heels of the eight-year-old New Economic Policy, during which with official toleration a capitalist, private-property mentality had been acquired by some of the rural population. The synchronization of phases of transformation thus emerges empirically as a crucial variable in accounting for variations in the intensity of terror in different countries.

A mixed pattern of reintegration occurred in Eastern Europe, with the regimes in Bulgaria, Rumania, and Hungary attempting, by design or necessity, partly to collectivize and at the same time to organize transitional cooperative structures. The extent of collectivization achieved reflected an interplay between the degree of violence applied and the degree of resistance manifested on the part of the peasantry.[10] As suggested, the result was widespread violence as the urban cadres clashed with the individualistic peasantry. In the post-Stalin years, however, direct coercion was de-emphasized, and the scope of collectivized agriculture was extended without recourse to overt terror. Lacking a systemic alternative but possessing a safety valve in the form of his private plot, the peasant succumbed to "creeping collectivization" as Communist administrative control in the countryside was extended, as hope for radical change faded, and as efforts were made to correct the previous insufficiency of capital investment in agriculture and of material incentives for the peasantry.[11]

---

[10] Korbonski, "The Agricultural Problem in East Central Europe," p. 76.

[11] Dellin, "Agriculture and the Peasant," pp. 75ff; James Brown, *The New Eastern Europe*, ch. 3.

The post-Stalin years first brought collectivization to a halt, with the 1956 crisis in Poland leading to the virtual disappearance of all collectives and in Hungary bringing about the temporary dissolution of many. From 1957 on, collectivization resumed at a more rapid pace, with Bulgaria and Czechoslovakia completing the process by 1958, and Hungary by 1961. Rumania proceeded more gradually until in 1962 collectivization was declared nominally (and fictitiously) complete. East Germany scored a breakthrough of intense transformation in 1960, characteristically with strong organizational development and discipline in the countryside.

This Eastern European approach involves, then, a partial disintegration followed by incremental reintegration, permitting
less than total war in the breakthrough phase and sharply
diminished violence thereafter. Such a multi-step approach
allows for practical retreats without requiring ideological compromise. Thus, when in 1951–52 the Rumanian leadership
found rural violence too costly, it could legitimately "decom-
press" by shifting its emphasis from higher- to lower-level cooperatives. But where the regime is wedded to a single organizational form, its options are considerably narrowed and the
need for terror is likely to be greater. In such a case concessions
can involve only modulations within the system—a temporary
slowing of the process, a reduction in compulsory deliveries, or
an enlargement of the private plot, for example. Of course, the
East European regimes had been able to learn from the earlier
experience of the Soviet Union and were apparently determined
to avoid it.

Nevertheless, even if the East European pattern made possible the avoidance of the "cult of the kolkhoz" and of the
degree of terror experienced by the Soviet Union, it can by no
means be considered a coherent model for agricultural development. As we shall see, the economic consequences of the early
violent push for collectivization were disastrous. Lack of investment in capital goods necessary for rural mechanization, the
antagonizing of an individualistic peasantry, brutal excesses on
the part of lower bureaucrats, and the suppression of the most
productive farmers—all these made the post-1953 correctives
more of a salvaging operation than part of a preconceived
strategy for partial disintegration and incremental reintegration. Nevertheless, it does appear that wholesale adoption of
the Soviet approach would have caused even greater dislocation.
Furthermore, a "kolkhoz cult" would not have allowed the sort
of organizational adjustments that were needed to determine
optimal farm size and adequate incentives for the peasants.[12]

[12] Moshe Lewin, in "The Immediate Background of Soviet Collectivization," also
stresses the extent to which the fixation upon a single organizational form caused determined peasant resistance.

Organizational Development

What we mean here by organizational development is the extent of the Communist party's administrative penetration of rural areas (including the network of machine-tractor stations), the technical and managerial skills of the cadres, the reliability of information flow between higher and lower levels of the party apparatus, and the degree of discipline of lower-level cadres. Everything else being equal, the higher the level of organizational development during the disintegration phase, the lower the level of coercion typically needed. A high level of organizational development tends to diminish "situational terror" by overly zealous administrators, to minimize peasant alienation thanks to the indigenous origins of the cadres, and to allow for controlled, incremental transition between phases of development. Furthermore, in the initial process of agrarian reform, greater organization may secure some popular support for the regime because selective control of a potentially chaotic process then becomes possible.

As suggested earlier, the expropriation of landlords in China served an "educative" function by breaking the economic and psychological hold of traditional authorities, demonstrating their vulnerability, and assuring that they would have no power in the future.[13] Since this controlled, systematic, but indirect process was made possible by the earlier experience of the party, the lower strata of the peasantry were not alienated from the Communist authorities at this stage, as they otherwise might have been. As one observer remarks,

Most important about the process of land reform for future social control was first the active participation of the populace and second the controlled use of terror. By directly and emotionally involving the masses in the process of change, by mobilizing them through their own will and giving them a share of the responsibility, the change was accepted positively, and a favorable attitude given to the regime that carried out that change. No Extraordinary Commissions [Cheka] came in and simply shot down landlords. Also critical for future stability was the policy of not attacking the middle peasantry.[14]

---

[13] See Schram, *Mao Tse-tung*, pp. 258–60.
[14] Gundersheim, "Terror and Political Control," p. 41.

The Russian Revolution, by contrast, was urban-based, with little administrative control of the countryside, and was followed by the turmoil of civil war. The initial land reform was a spontaneous process, carried out by a euphoric and at times anarchic peasantry that was loyal to the regime only insofar as it was willing to countenance the process and to protect newly won property from restoration to the former owners. Indeed, the ruthless requisitioning carried out by urban and armed bands thoroughly antagonized the peasantry. In sum, the relative lack of organizational development significantly affected the level of violence employed in later stages of agrarian transformation.

Similarly, the extent of situational terror during the reintegration phase appears to be inversely related to the level of organizational development. In China a gradualist policy was made possible by continuous recruitment and training of cadres, and "the organizational base in the villages ... [which] provided the information on local conditions that made selective mobilization [of those least likely to resist] possible."[15] But if it is correct that the "weaker and more inexperienced the village leaders and the larger and more complex the new collectives" the greater the coercion,[16] then the degree of synchronization of phases appears to be a more decisive variable than the level of organizational development. Thus, the Chinese village was able to minimize coercion only when the number of specific tasks it was charged with was relatively limited and when the span of control of the individual cadre was not very great.

Nevertheless, these variables interact in determining the level of terror. Little organizational development may cause considerable situational terror even when tasks are clearly specified and phases are carried out separately. For example, dekulakization in the Soviet Union, even when carried out apart from collectivization, elicited extensive terror on the part of a brutal, undisciplined administrative bureaucracy.[17] Conversely, cruel excesses (on a much lesser scale than the Soviet, to be sure) occurred

---

[15] Bernstein, "Leadership and Mass Mobilization," p. 37.
[16] *Ibid.*, p. 16.
[17] Lewin, *Russian Peasants and Soviet Power*, p. 499.

in China during the rapid push to full cooperativization in 1955–56. In this situation, organizational discipline could not overcome the pressures placed on the cadres.

It is true that the Chinese gradualism ended abruptly in 1958. Communization, as the rural counterpart of the Great Leap Forward, entailed a radical change in the pattern of rural life and organization. Where the Great Leap was implemented, private property was made communal, private life gave way to communal living, and the rural masses were grouped into military-type organizations for an all-out assault on nature. The result was a "general atmosphere of regimentation and 'militarization.' "[18] Communization was carried out through coercive mobilization combined with "socialist education" and the promise of economic abundance to come. Compliance was thus based on a combination of coercive, normative, and "deferred" material power—compliance on credit, as it were. Thus "to a significant extent the enthusiasm of poor and lower-middle peasants for free supply and instant modernization swept rural China to the threshold of communism. Or so at least it seemed."[19]

Although the use of terror during the Great Leap Forward was restrained compared to the Soviet experience with radical transformation, it was not negligible. Captured documents tell of "brute terror" perpetrated by "ill-trained or corrupt" cadres; "dictatorial leaders in the rural areas took command of peasant groups and army units and grossly mishandled the mounting chaos set in motion by the Great Leap Forward."[20] These documents indicate that the organizational discipline of the cadres had either deteriorated significantly or had never really been as tight as had been believed. Of course, objective circumstances related to the speed and scope of transformation and the level of organizational development may have created a situation in which the more ruthless personalities among the cadres could find an outlet for their tendencies. For one thing, the sud-

[18] Barnett, *Cadres, Bureaucracy, and Political Power in Communist China*, p. 338.
[19] Skinner and Winckler, "Compliance Succession in Rural Communist China," p. 431.
[20] John Lewis, "China's Secret Military Papers," p. 74.

den shift to total transformation—the sudden abandoning of any measure of gradualism—provided opportunities for the summary punishment of wavering peasants and for the settling of old scores. For another, the sudden widening of the span of control of individual cadres made patience and persuasion less probable: "The effective cadre forces of the Party were very thinly spread in view of the enormous multiplication of individual enterprises in the communes.[21]

Nevertheless, purposive physical violence was minimal and apparently unnecessary for achieving rapid mobilization of the masses. Once again, this was apparently related to organizational development and synchronization of phases. There was no longer any organized opposition; and the earlier

killings [of landlords had left] a lasting imprint on the attitudes of everyone, including the ordinary peasants; it impressed upon them the power of the new regime and its capacity to use arbitrary and extreme violence, if and when it wished, against all persons classified as enemies of the state.[22]

Hence, unlike the Soviet collectivization, where disintegration of traditional ties and transformation of rural organization were simultaneous processes, an even more extreme transformation in China required little violence, largely because disintegration had been carried out earlier and in a manner that had provided the regime with a legitimacy not possessed by its Soviet counterpart.

Moreover, securing popular compliance during the Great Leap was facilitated by the extensive administrative network in the countryside. The villagers knew "that the communists' instruments of political power [were] an ever-present and inescapable reality."[23] By now, in short, all options other than compliance or futile resistance had been effectively eliminated; it was another characteristic example of the totalitarian technique of depriving the population of alternatives.[24] But the ex-

---

[21] Joseph Peterson, *The Great Leap—China*, p. 267. Peterson is not discussing terror in communization; nor does he in general stress coercive aspects of the Great Leap.
[22] Barnett, *Cadres, Bureaucracy, and Political Power*, p. 229.
[23] *Ibid.*, p. 389.
[24] "There was hardly much enthusiasm in the villages for these burdensome tasks.

haustive regimentation and lack of economic incentives soon
led to disillusionment among the peasant masses; as elsewhere,
they turned to the only forms of resistance possible: foot-dragging and dissimulation. In some areas, however, the hunger
and brutality of the later stages of the commune experiment
sparked armed peasant revolts that were decisively suppressed
by the People's Liberation Army.[25]

In the Soviet case, the low level of rural organization[26] meant
that few cadres had the skills necessary for leadership and
mobilization. Stalin's use of the purge against inexperienced
and often undisciplined cadres, moreover, led to widespread
falsification of information and coercion on their part, as lower
units often vied with each other to demonstrate their "socialist
fervor." Thus the overwhelming tasks and the severe penalties
for failure, both actual and anticipated, contributed to bureaucratic excesses.[27]

In Eastern Europe, too, the weakness of organizational development made situational terror a frequent occurrence in
most of the Communist systems that pressed ahead with collectivization. Typically, because of the shortage of cadres and the
low level of discipline, local administrators had relatively great
operational autonomy. In addition, the local authorities charged
with "liquidating the kulak" (and the term was defined even
more vaguely here than in Russia) tended to interpret elite goals
very loosely, often (as in the Soviet Union) pinning the kulak
label on anyone who resisted the transformation.

Charged with destroying the kulaks and simultaneously with
setting up cooperatives and collectives, local cadres typically
vied with each other in forcing peasants into higher-level organizations. As a result, foot-dragging and sabotage on the part

---

But by this time the whole rural Party apparatus had been mobilized to make sure that
the peasants developed the requisite 'positivism' for irrigation labor." (Schurmann, *Ideology and Organization in Communist China*, p. 466.)

[25] Lewis, "China's Secret Military Papers."

[26] On the eve of collectivization in Russia 40 per cent of villages had party cells; in
China 90 per cent of *hsiang* did. (Bernstein, "Leadership and Mass Mobilization,"
pp. 7–8.)

[27] This in turn may well have reinforced the vicious circle wherein the elites revise
their goals upward, on the basis of optimistic but false information passed up from the
grass roots.

of the peasants lowered the productivity of established cooperatives, thus further lowering the economic inducement for other peasants to join voluntarily. And so the cycle of stagnation and repression went on, until the regime had either to slow down the transformation or opt for more coercion. At the same time, liquidating the kulaks meant eliminating those most vigorously opposed to giving up their farms and produce—namely, the most skilled and productive farmers. This, of course, could only contribute further to general economic stagnation in the countryside.[28]

Elite Values and Perceptions

In assessing the roots of terror in the countryside, we must not ignore the role of elite values.[29] An explanation of the severity of collectivization in Bulgaria, for instance, requires some understanding of the country's and the Communist elite's commitment to look to Russia—and to Stalin, in fact—for guidance; at the same time there was an ubiquitous determination on the part of non-Soviet elites to limit the use of violence in order to avoid the degree of chaos and violence experienced in Russia in 1930–34. Similarly, the intensity of the Hungarian upheaval must be seen against the background of Mátyás Rákosi's hegemony at home and his determination to prove himself as Stalin's most orthodox and zealous lieutenant. In the case of China, the distinctive strategy of agrarian transformation and the concern with "voluntarism" derived in part from values acquired during the civil war years, and in part from the lessons learned from the Soviet experience.[30] As for Stalin himself, he

[28] For some vivid illustrations, see Korbonski, *Politics of Socialist Agriculture in Poland 1945–1960*.

[29] For the view that Communist cadres, who "made no bones about their contempt for the peasantry, which they regarded as an essentially reactionary class," had absorbed the anti-peasant bias of the pre-1939 ruling elites in Eastern Europe, see Korbonski, "The Agricultural Problem," p. 75.

[30] For Liu Shao-ch'i's argument of why, for economic reasons, it was important to "preserve the rich peasant economy," see his speech, "On the Agrarian Reform Law," June 1950, to the National Committee of the People's Political Consultative Conference. In it he also discussed the "deviations" in seizing the land and property of rich peasants that had occurred in north and northeast China in 1946–47 (including "cases of indiscriminate beatings and killings"), attributing them mainly to "the serious political and military situation at that time" and the lack of experience of Communist rural cadres. As Ezra Vogel comments, "Having studied Soviet affairs very closely, [Liu] was

neither knew nor understood the peasantry; he was prepared to ride roughshod over all resistance, and, having gravely misjudged the situation, he was able to delay and relax but a little, being profoundly committed to striving for what he saw as higher goals even if it cost millions of lives and widespread privation.

The differential perception of economic conditions and the priority of development goals also makes for significant variations in the use of coercive power. Mao and Liu knew, for instance, that China was too close to the subsistence level to be able to afford Soviet-style collectivization even if they had wanted to attempt it. Moreover, the difference in strategies toward industrialization had its effect. Whereas Stalin needed to have farm production "finance" industrialization quickly, in China industrialization was a lesser goal, usually subordinated to ideological aims;[31] in Eastern Europe industrialization had been achieved to some extent before collectivization and was partly circumscribed by extraneous pressures.[32]

Thus we find that terror assumed the forms of total elimination and direct coercion in the Soviet Union, where the elite had no model of development to refer to in calculating costs, and where the leader was a willful, ruthless dictator determined to "succeed"—speedily and at any cost save the stability of the polity and his rule. Synchronization of tasks followed the alienation of the lower and middle peasant strata and the entrenchment of the richer peasants. These elements contributed to the leader's commitment to a single, "advanced" form of agricul-

---

well aware of the difficulties resulting from the liquidation of the kulaks" (cited in Gundersheim, "Terror and Political Control," p. 35). See also C. K. Yang, *A Chinese Village in Early Communist Transition.*

[31] Including the development of "relations of production" before the "forces of production."

[32] We take for granted the relevance of additional variables that cannot be investigated here. Ideological constraints may properly be subsumed under elite values. Foreign constraints are exemplified by the close parallelism of East European and Soviet zigzags of policy. Lewin (*Russian Peasants,* p. 483) gives an example of pertinent cultural components in discussing two types of personnel involved in Soviet dekulakization and collectivization: on the one hand, those who had served in the Red Army during the civil war and could easily be given the signal to "go ahead and behave as they had been accustomed to behaving"; and, on the other hand, particularly in the rural areas, "the typical Russian *derzhimorda,* brutal, ignorant, and rapacious. These two types of bureaucrat, both widely represented in the government apparatus, were virtually given a free hand."

tural organization, a circumstance that, coupled with the low level of organizational development, further increased peasant resistance and in turn multiplied terror and abuse.

The cost of these policies in terms of the losses suffered was enormous; seldom was any government to wreak such havoc on its own country. Having no alternative program or position on which to fall back, the government neither could nor would see any way out, other than to exert further pressure, and to carry on with collectivization.[33]

In China, by contrast, the elite was more flexible and more at home with the problems of the countryside; it pursued a policy of systematic disintegration in which terror was used far more selectively to secure both compliance and legitimacy—a policy made possible in part by the higher level of organizational development. The regime's policy differed strikingly from the Soviet, and it evidently succeeded in the 1950's in gaining the support of the poor peasantry rather than alienating it. In China, moreover, disintegration preceded reintegration to a greater extent; and as a result the administrative apparatus was not overburdened. Until the Great Leap, reintegration tended to be incremental and relatively nonviolent, terror less frequent, less diffuse, and characteristically linked with normative appeals.

The question remains whether there are other options that Communist systems committed to the ultimate transformation of the countryside could pursue if they chose to avoid extreme terror and disruption. The Polish experience so far suggests an unstable equilibrium rather than an alternative model, but the discussion among specialists there, as elsewhere in Eastern Europe, has elicited some interesting ideas.[34] The Yugoslav experience is in many ways more viable but presupposes a greater degree of popular commitment than was the case either in Russia or in most of Eastern Europe on the eve of collectivization. The principle of voluntary and autonomous cooperatives, of

[33] Lewin, *Russian Peasants*, pp. 515–16.
[34] See, for example, Korbonski, "Peasant Agriculture in Socialist Poland since 1956: An Alternative to Collectivization."

course, virtually precludes the application of political terror.[35] In the Soviet Union most of the leaders other than Stalin— and most notably, Nikolai Bukharin—had insisted on the necessity and the possibility of rational gradualism in rural transformation. Indeed, Stalin himself had been hesitant to opt for the cataclysmic terror that engulfed the countryside in 1929–33.[36] In retrospect, it seems probable, furthermore, that with a good deal of advance preparation in terms of investments, agronomic assistance, imports, and organizational development a viable cooperative sector could have been created in the Soviet countryside, without extreme coercion, much less terror.[37] To be sure, this kind of preparation would have required that the elite focus its attention on issues other than the power struggle; it might also have caused ideological strain in the CPSU, which was anything but peasant-oriented. Yet these were circumstances characteristic of a specific case, and they indicate that the entire Soviet experience cannot be generalized to other polities. Except for their influence on post-Stalin elites, especially in Eastern Europe, the possible options that might have been pursued in the Soviet Union remain in the realm of might-have-been's. But they do suggest that, although the system made the specifics of Stalinist policy possible, it did not make them inevitable.

A final question relates to the political consequences of agrarian transformation terror. One Communist leader, who has consistently opposed collectivization, sees the Soviet pattern in retrospect as "the beginning of the process of growing lawlessness . . . the establishment of an atmosphere of fear, and the growth on this foundation of the personality cult," presumably as a prelude to the Great Purge.[38] Such a linkage must remain speculative, but both theory and empirical evidence lend support to this thesis. A process of radical, coercive change is bound

[35] See, for example, Edvard Kardelj, *Problemi socijalističke politike na selu*; George Hoffman and Fred Neal, *Yugoslavia*; Charles McVicker, *Titoism*, ch. 6. See also Michael Gamarnikow, *Economic Reforms in Eastern Europe*, pp. 159–74.
[36] See Nove, *Economic Rationality*. See also Lewin, "The Immediate Background."
[37] Lewin, "The Immediate Background," p. 193.
[38] Wladyslaw Gomulka, Report to the Central Committee of the PUWP, Nov. 22, 1961, trans. in Alexander Dallin et al., eds., *Diversity in International Communism*, pp. 325–26.

to be carried out by organizations that develop a vested interest in secrecy, suspicion, and the "uncovering" of enemies. The result, when coupled with the syndrome of high coercion begetting low or distorted information,[39] is likely to be a greater suspicion on the part of a more isolated elite that enemies abound. Such a situation paves the way to labeling all opposition seditious and equating all dissent with treason.

Furthermore, controversial policies of radical change are bound to cause conflict within the elite. Regardless of the objective success or failure of a policy, widespread terror or disruption will often cause squabbles that may seriously jeopardize a leader's authority. Stalin was almost voted out of office in 1932 in reaction to the violence of collectivization. Similarly, it has been suggested that the failure of the Great Leap seriously undermined Mao's authority; it caused lasting policy conflicts within the elite that may well have contributed to the bitterness of the Cultural Revolution.[40] It is entirely possible, then, that both the Great Purge and the Cultural Revolution were partly motivated by Stalin's and Mao's desire to avoid "side-payments"[41] to dissenting members of their political elite.

Mobilization: A Review

At the mobilization stage all Communist regimes have resorted to terror for assuring political control and for facilitating the socioeconomic transformation of the countryside. Their experiences bear out the view that differences in speed and sequence in the various phases of directed social change make for significant differences in outcome.

The Soviet Union in the 1930's epitomizes the attempt to mobilize simultaneously all three kinds of assets—normative, material, and coercive—and accordingly to incur high costs and great strains that were further heightened by the irrational ex-

---

[39] See Apter, *Politics of Modernization, passim.* See also pp. 82–83, below.

[40] See Tsou, "Revolution, Reintegration, and Crisis in Communist China," in Ho and Tsou, I, 321ff.

[41] For the concept of "side-payments," see R. M. Cyert and J. G. March, *A Behavioral Theory of the Firm*; for an imaginative application of the concept to coalition-building in Communist and other developing polities, see Kenneth Jowitt, "A Comparative Analysis of Leninist and Nationalist Elite Ideologies and Nation-Building Strategies."

tension of the purge. In substance, here were the tensions caused
by general mobilization:

(1) the mobilization of material assets was meant to spur production and increase the national product—but it inevitably
conflicted with the simultaneous need to provide more material
incentives to bring such an effort about, with the latter objective
losing out as a result;

(2) the mobilization of all normative resources, including
mass media and all agencies of socialization, was meant to
cushion the great exertion—but was severely handicapped because the process of mobilizing coercive and material resources
had considerably shrunk the regime's "reserves" of normative
power; the popular reaction to the combination of pervasive
terror and inadequate material conditions reduced support for
the regime;

(3) the mobilization of coercive assets—monopolizing the
agencies of coercion in the system—and their ready activation
reflected the leader's perception of the need to rely heavily on
compulsion to harness an increasingly inert (or, to use Chalmers Johnson's term, "nonrevolutionary") population, which
responded sluggishly or worse to policies that, it was widely
surmised, were likely to heighten its own deprivation and insecurity; but the scope and methods of terror and purges in turn
handicapped the regime's quest for legitimacy.

Since the total mobilization of coercive and material assets
is intrinsically incompatible with the total mobilization of
normative assets, at least a partial "retreat," in at least one
sector, must occur. If economic growth and the development of
political institutions remain among the priority goals of the
regime, logically a certain decrease in the level of coercion and
perhaps in the integrating role of Communist organization and
ideology should follow. But this is a dilemma Stalin left un-
resolved along with other problems he bequeathed to his successors.

The regimes of the derivative Communist polities in Eastern
Europe found it even harder than the Soviet leadership to

6 The Post-Mobilization Stage

The eradicating of the long-standing system of terror was
the nation's first and foremost need.

Svetlana Alliluyeva

As Communist systems pass beyond the mobilization stage, the
incidence of political terror as an instrument of public policy
tends to decline sharply. Although the empirical evidence on
this trend is still slim—some Communist polities, such as China
and Cuba, have not reached this stage, and others are still in a
phase of somewhat uncertain transition—it is apparent that at
the post-mobilization stage the tendency toward the disuse of
political terror is congruent with other changes in the system
that together characterize the dynamics of the post-mobilization
stage.

Political terror may well persist in a variety of ways—as a
diffuse anxiety based on the lively memory of the earlier period;
as the *ultima ratio* that remains available to the state; or as the
residual product of surviving institutions and processes of
coercion (as indeed it remains, latent or manifest, in all societies). Nevertheless, the dramatic change that typically occurs
at this stage is one of kind, not just of degree. Such a change may
come about in three ways. Calculable forms of coercion may be
substituted for arbitrary forms; this is seen, for example, in the
role of the judicial system and legal norms, the routine tasks of
the uniformed police, and various (at times, less predictable)
forms of social pressure and public intimidation. There may
occur a shift in the balance among the three alternative sanction
systems and, more specifically, a relatively greater reliance on
normative and material power than on coercive power. Finally,
the total scope of political control or the assets expended for it
by the ruling elite may decrease. One or more of these processes

may be involved in the rearrangement of the political-control system at this stage.

The changes relevant to the fate of political terror are outcomes, either desired or unintended, of the prior forced-modernization process or of earlier policy choices. Thus, at the mobilization stage, the elite aims at a fundamental transformation of socioeconomic relations and of individual human nature, whereas at the post-mobilization stage it tends to realize that economic development has become increasingly self-sustaining and no longer dependent on inefficient coercive mobilization. Finally, whatever its rhetoric,[1] the elite tends in practice to end up neglecting or ignoring other transformation objectives previously accepted as ideologically "given."[2] One may posit, moreover, that all industrial societies tend to require or ultimately generate a stable matrix of role expectations.[3]

Whereas at the mobilization stage, as we have seen, Communist policy-makers may resort to social prophylaxis and the system-wide institutionalization of universal suspicion, at the subsequent stage entire social strata are no longer eliminated or isolated. On the one hand, the regime and society now tend toward a "substantial consensus";[4] on the other, no more transformation breakthroughs are contemplated or attempted.[5] Moreover the greater resource base that has meanwhile developed makes possible a partial shift from coercive power to material power, or incentives, while the socialization process vigorously promoted by the regime presumably assures enough acquiescence to make possible a similar shift toward normative power. Especially in instances where the shift in policy follows a change in leadership or evidence of the leaders' good faith,

[1] See Tucker, "The Deradicalization of Marxist Movements."

[2] In Chalmers Johnson's terms, the "goal culture" is silently abandoned as the "ideology" is transformed into a stable system of values. See "Comparing Communist Nations," in Johnson, ed., *Change in Communist Systems.*

[3] See Moore, *Terror and Progress—USSR*, pp. 190ff; and Dahrendorf, *Essays in the Theory of Society, passim.*

[4] Friedrich, "Totalitarianism: Recent Trends," p. 34.

[5] The Eastern European experience does not entirely conform to this "ideal type," since collectivization in most countries took place in the post-1956 period. These years can properly be considered a "twilight phase" before the derivative systems fully passed beyond the stage of coercive mobilization.

even previously alienated elements of the population may be willing to give the new leaders a chance to promote precisely the kinds of changes likely to increase the regime's legitimacy.

Still, terror as an instrument of purposive policy does not erode or wither "on its own," even as a consequence of systemic changes. The decline in its use requires active or passive, explicit or tacit, decision-making. Whether, when, or in what form in a given polity such decisions are made cannot be predicted; but it may be hypothesized that the necessary preconditions for such a change are typically created as part of the transition just described. In essence, the decision-makers' assessment of the possibility or necessity of dispensing with the use of political terror depends on a combination of events at the time, elite perception, and elite priorities. Changes in these factors may be expected to bring about a changed assessment of the relative costs and benefits of political terror.

Thus the elite, and to an even greater extent, the increasingly articulate corpus of experts, now tend to put a higher premium on criteria of regularity and predictability, such as legal norms and procedures. As Max Weber wrote,

Bureaucratization offers above all the optimum possibility for carrying through the principle of specializing administrative functions according to purely objective considerations.... The "objective" discharge of business primarily means a discharge of business according to *calculable rules*, and "without regard to persons." ... The peculiarity of modern culture, and specifically of its technical and economic basis, demands this very "calculability" of results.[6]

Likewise, the elite typically gives greater weight than it earlier did to considerations of economic efficiency, to the rationalization of production, distribution, and administration, and to technological and scientific innovation. It is also likely to be more aware of the inverse relationship between information and coercion. The need for a freer flow of objective information "upward" is now likely to be perceived more keenly, as there

---

[6] Max Weber, *Wirtschaft und Gesellschaft*, trans. in Gerth and Mills, *From Max Weber: Essays in Sociology*, p. 215.

is likely to be greater recognition that political terror, because it paralyzes the information flow, tends to make an objective assessment of the system's operation doubly difficult.[7]

In any polity, as the structure of society changes in the course of modernization, there tend to be greater role specialization and interest aggregation. At this stage many of the arguments of informal subgroups tend to be mutually reinforcing in their negative attitude toward mass terror. A part of the creative intelligentsia may advocate a greater concern for socialist "humanism"; military men may be more conscious of or more outspoken about the consequences of political terror for military competence and capabilities; managerial personnel, planners, and scientists may be more keenly aware of the costs of terror in economic growth, the waste of skilled manpower and scarce resources, and the inhibition of innovation and invention.

Thus the political elite, increasingly obliged or willing to recognize such attitudes, is likely to reevaluate the use of terror in terms of changing elite priorities; and, weighing the costs of terror as it knows them against the possible costs of doing without terror as it foresees them, if it feels secure enough it is likely to opt for a drastic reduction in the use of terror.[8] Moreover, various civilian and military groups, once they are able to express themselves candidly, may be expected to point to the threat represented by the continuing institutional autonomy of the secret-police empire and to the debilitating consequences of the diffuse anxiety that may still pervade the society.

At least in indigenous Communist polities, a crucial part of the leadership's thinking is likely to be its perception that political socialization has progressed to the point where the regime's legitimacy may be taken for granted. Because "more and more citizens have obviously accepted the values of the regime as their own, the Party can rely more . . . on peer-group

---

[7] See Apter, *The Politics of Modernization*; Friedrich and Brzezinski, *Totalitarian Dictatorship and Autocracy*, p. 129; Moore, *Terror and Progress*, p. 170.

[8] The choice need not be so explicit: it may well be existential and incremental; but the ingredients are likely to be those suggested above. Moreover, if the transition to the post-mobilization stage is accompanied by, or is the consequence of, a change in leadership, the successors may be eager to dispel any "guilt by association" as heirs to a regime widely identified with the use of political terror.

pressure" and can substitute "majority tyranny" for overt terror.[9] Under such conditions decision-makers typically conclude that political terror—manifested as the physical extermination of individuals and groups, without due process or cause, and with pervasive popular anxiety as its outcome—has become, or threatens to become, counterproductive.[10] Although such a conclusion and its "organizational consequences" are likely to be resisted by some elements within the elite, either because of ideological and bureaucratic rigidity or because of their own vested interests, the trend toward pluralism in the elite and in the society militates for a decline in the use of terror.

After Stalin

The experiences of the Soviet Union and Eastern Europe show that whereas in the post-Stalin years there was indeed a striking change in the use of political terror, the transition to a new stage may itself be a drawn-out process full of zigzags, ambiguities, and contradictions.

The fact of Stalin's disappearance as an authority figure had a powerful liberating effect on his successors, making it virtually impossible for any of them to use or risk using physical violence against intra-elite rivals.[11] Those who favored a drastic cut in the role of the secret police and the use of coercive measures were fortunate that a broad coalition so promptly agreed on the forcible removal of Beria, for this action led to the extensive dismantling of the terror apparatus and the subordination of the security services to the party; it was also important for the

[9] Meyer, *The Soviet Political System*, pp. 331–32. One may of course conceive of situations in which the counterproductive, alienating consequences of terror in the mobilization stage are so disastrous as to preclude the production of such support. By the same token, such a regime may or may not have successfully achieved, or abandoned, its "transfer goal," which we posit as a condition for the transition beyond the mobilization stage. A more balanced allocation of resources to multiple goals is the process that distinguishes the post-mobilization stage.

[10] Terror may or may not have been dysfunctional at a much earlier point, without this circumstance having been perceived, much less acted upon by a committed leader.

[11] Dahl has argued that "the prospects of successful coercion decline when opposition groups improve their own opportunities to resort to defensive violence if they are threatened with coercion." One of the key factors in the transition to nonviolent political relations between government and opposition is their perception of the "limited preponderance of coercive forces" available to the government. The implication is that tolerance of political opposition increases as available instruments of force, such as police and army, become weaker and as the perceived threat to the government lessens. (*Political Oppositions in Western Democracies*, pp. xiii–xiv.)

satellite countries, for it triggered a similar weakening of Soviet
security control in Eastern Europe. Although the Beria affair
was but a specific expression of the elite's insecurity, it had
significant systemic consequences; in fact, it is hard to think of
other circumstances that could have been equally effective in
creating the preconditions for the changes in the role of terror
that ensued in the following decade. But the underlying trends
followed essentially the pattern outlined on the preceding pages.

Some of the major trends of the Khrushchev era were the
rejection of Stalinism, an attempt to foster an ideological revival, and what the Maoists were to assail as "economism," i.e.
the priority of economic over political goals. Functionally, all
three were inversely related to the use of terror. Reacting to the
experience of the Stalin era, at least some leaders thought terror
had exacted what now seemed an excessive price: a paralyzing
atomization of society reflecting its members' fears of communi-
cating with one another, diffuse anxiety within the elite as well
as throughout the population, and a stifling of creativity and
candor. They tried now to kindle a new utopian commitment
with greater stress on participation, on voluntary (even extralegal) administrative and control mechanisms, mirroring the alleged beginnings of "withering" state institutions, as the system
ostensibly moved toward the higher stage of Communism. The
new leadership responded likewise to the pressures for decen-
tralization in administration and to a lesser extent in economic
planning, pressures for autonomy in management, for encouragement of controlled initiative and innovation, and for a style
of experimentation that presupposed some tolerance of error
and failure. All of these goals were incompatible with reliance
on terror. Furthermore, the new concern with such values as
efficiency, rationality, and predictability, even if logically incompatible with some of the above ends, also worked against
the persistence of terror.[12]

In brief, the Soviet Union since 1956 has witnessed four sig-

---

[12] Among accounts of the Khrushchev era, see, for example, Fainsod, *How Russia Is
Ruled*, pp. 447 *et seq.*, and his "Transformations in the Communist Party of the Soviet
Union"; Leonhard, *The Kremlin After Stalin*; and Michel Tatu, *Power in the Kremlin*.
On the changing role of ideology, see Kurt Marko, *Evolution wider Willen*.

nificant, albeit inconsistently implemented, changes with regard
to coercion: the abatement of coercive mobilization; the disappearance of diffuse violence as transformation breakthroughs
are no longer attempted; the de facto disappearance of atomization thanks to both the objective constraints that society has
begun to impose on the organs of government and the lessen-
ing of anxiety in interpersonal relations; and the halting, zig-
zagging, but dominant tendency to move from a highly prescriptive system to an essentially restrictive one. The significance
of these changes must not be underrated even if there have been
—and no doubt will be—powerful efforts to stem and reverse
the trend. Most of the forced-labor camps have been emptied
and abandoned, though some are still in existence. Many secret-
police officials have been replaced or purged, and some of the
former functions of the MGB and MVD have been transferred
to other agencies, even though the secret police as an institution
continues in active existence. Many prominent victims of the
Stalin era have been rehabilitated, but others have not been
cleared of spurious charges. There have been remarkable ex-
pressions of independent opinion, yet the habits of Stalinist
rhetoric have proved disturbingly tenacious, and instances of
political persecution continue and have in fact again multiplied
since Khrushchev's ouster in 1964.

Even if the regime has continued to feel a need to reaffirm its
traditional commitment to unanimity, even if Khrushchev as
well as his successors have felt impelled time and again to
threaten, cajole, and inveigh against dissident intellectuals, even
if the bureaucracy still frequently exhibits a total intolerance
of nonconformity, the critical facts in sharp contrast with the
earlier era are that the compliant mass of the population has
become generally immune from terror, and that even in regard
to its recent victims coercion, however distasteful, has generally
been fairly predictable rather than arbitrary.

It may be well here to remind ourselves of our initial definition of terror as a policy of severe and arbitrary coercion or its
credible threat. We find in recent Soviet practice the substitution of selective intimidation and penalization for mass terror,

along with widespread uncertainty about the likely scope and the credibility of threats of further coercion. In the post-Khrushchev years severe coercion has indeed been applied once again more visibly and apparently more widely, but it has been directed largely against certain well-defined zones of society, such as dissidents among the cultural intelligentsia and particular ethnic minorities—essentially, those suspected of being carriers of incongruent values. With some exceptions, the victims of the new repression have usually been aware of the risks they have taken, say, by sending manuscripts to be published abroad or by protesting against the Soviet occupation of Czechoslovakia.

Whereas terror continues to be felt by some citizens, it is no longer a means of general public policy. No doubt there are significant variations in the way different people perceive the situation. Some are intimidated by threats and by examples of deterrent action. "Here, too, memory plays a key role, leading many people to exaggerate the intensity of threats and to assume that they are intended to apply broadly rather than narrowly even when this is not the case."[13] Yet other people have evidently been able to adapt themselves rather successfully to the new conditions.[14] Ironically, some of the anxiety of the post-Stalin period was—especially in the 1950's—experienced by the former perpetrators of terror. Opportunistic informers probably saw in the change of policy highlighted by Khrushchev's "secret" speech to the Twentieth Congress an invitation to their victims to return to haunt—or stalk—them.[15]

There remains, it is true, a serious "credibility gap" between threat and action, an uncertainty that engenders insecurity in Soviet society because in large measure the regime is unable or

[13] Azrael, "Is Coercion Withering Away?" p. 16. It seems to us that to speak of community pressure as "decentralized violence" and of "psychic pressure" as the forms of terror on which the Soviet regime has come to rely (Friedrich, "Totalitarianism: Recent Trends," pp. 39–40) is, in one case, to invoke a phenomenon scarcely comparable in scale, manipulability, and impact, and in the other, to substitute a semantic redundancy.

[14] This has obvious implications for the efficacy of political control through the use of coercive assets: the more remote the Stalin period becomes in popular consciousness, the greater the investment of normative and material assets evidently required for the maintenance of political control. After all, "It is no use employing Stalinist methods of intimidation at a time when most people, particularly the younger generation, have lost the conditioned reflexes induced by Stalinist terror." (Max Hayward, "Introduction," in Hayward and Labedz, *Literature and Revolution in the Soviet Union*, p. xx.)

[15] See, for example, the panicky reaction to these events attributed to Rusanov, in Solzhenitsyn's *The Cancer Ward*, pp. 173–96.

unwilling to define the boundaries of tolerance and deviance. But this very lack of definition also provides opportunities that some people have taken advantage of to voice unorthodox ideas. The system continues in a state of tension between the powerful pressures to adjust, tolerate, and let live, and the recurrent impulse to clamp down, enforce, and control. The former goes hand in hand with the abnegation of terror: it means precisely the kind of ambiguity tolerance that is tantamount to the maturation of the system as it grows out of its "infantile disease" of totalitarianism. Yet the dynamics of the situation are such that perversely the diminishing of fear, especially on the part of the oldest and youngest generations, who feel they have the least to lose, stimulates the expression of nonconformity and dissent—in works of art, in private and group petitions, in manuscripts circulated but not officially published, in manifestations of a deviant youth culture, and occasionally but rarely in public demonstrations—that in turn tempts officials committed to law and order (as they see them) to respond with a "backlash" of greater retribution.

In this regard Soviet domestic policy toward members of the intelligentsia and toward spokesmen of certain sectarian and ethnic groups has paralleled Soviet vacillation between toleration of diversity and violent enforcement of conformity in Eastern Europe. Many of the "liberal" currents of the Khrushchev era proved remarkably easy to reverse. And the techniques employed to deal with dissent—such as "political justice," confinement in mental institutions, exile from specified places of residence, threats of dismissal from employment, and public intimidation—are at times unmistakably terroristic in their impact.[16]

If then some real terror persists, it is nonetheless a very different phenomenon from the earlier Reign of Terror. Even in the

---

[16] On the harassment of nonconformist intellectuals since 1965, see, for example, Tatu, *Power in the Kremlin*; Tatu, "In Quest of Justice"; Alexander Werth, *Russia, Hopes and Fears*; a book by an anonymous author, "Observer," *Message from Moscow*; Anatoli Marchenko, *My Testimony*; Hayward and Labedz, eds., *On Trial*; Vyacheslav Chornovil, *The Chornovil Papers*; Alexander Ginzburg, comp., *Belaia kniga po delu A. Sinyavskogo i Yu. Danielia*; Ivan Dzyuba, *Internationalism or Russification?*; Karel van het Reve, comp., *Dear Comrade*; and Pavel Litvinov, *The Demonstration in Pushkin Square*.

grimmer years since 1965, coercion has been restricted and predictable as a rule. But so long as terror survives as a practice, backed by institutions, traditions, and ideological rationales, it is proper to wonder whether it might once again grow to "Stalinist" proportions. While a new Reign of Terror cannot be entirely ruled out, we believe it to be highly unlikely, for all the reasons that we have sought to adduce in this chapter. More particularly, spokesmen of all significant institutional and professional groups are intent on not again giving the police a free hand. Members of the elite would scarcely wish to gamble on their own survival if they permitted a new snowballing of terror. And, with all its vacillation, the leadership seems determined to contain the scope of terror so as to minimize its costs to the system as a whole.

In Eastern Europe, the analogous process began as a "derivative" echo of the Soviet changes; but indigenous and autonomous elements soon asserted themselves, especially as Soviet control weakened.[17] Most dramatically, the process was marked by attempted riots, revolts, and revolutions, consequences of a situation in which terror was scarcely used but the regimes had not gained much legitimacy. Terror may generate alienation, and the abandonment of terror may paradoxically permit the expression of such alienation in the form of organized resistance or revolt, or more mildly in various forms of civil dissent. In Eastern Europe most regimes have been faced with this dilemma.

Terror, Authority, and Stability

What are some of the unintended consequences for the stability of Communist systems of policy choices leading to the

---

[17] In Yugoslavia the leadership—before Stalin's death—chose to desist from political terror, not because "objective conditions" (such as substantial industrialization) forced it, but because of the general relaxation made possible by the legitimacy it enjoyed, made necessary (in its view) by exogenous circumstances, and made desirable by its effort to present Yugoslavia as the paragon of undeformed socialism. On this point, see also Lowenthal, in Johnson, *Change in Communist Systems*. Another suggestive perspective on developments in Eastern Europe is Skilling, "Background to the Study of Opposition in Communist Eastern Europe."

decompression of political control and the disuse of terror? Here the distinction between intra-elite behavior and mass patterns of behavior becomes important.

The decline in the use of terror was a precondition for such intra-elite challenges to the incumbent leadership as that of the so-called "anti-party group" against Khrushchev in June 1957, the successful challenge to Khrushchev in October 1964, and the replacement of Antonín Novotný by Alexander Dubček in January 1968. If after the execution of Beria and his associates the new pattern of quiet retirement of defeated leaders was welcome to those involved, it also reduced the risks of vying for power. Whether or not the assurance of survival results in a stronger tendency toward collective leadership or more frequent changes in leadership is an open question. But it is probably true that

the elimination of violence as the decisive instrumentality of political competition—a move that was perhaps prompted by the greater institutional maturity of Soviet society, and which was in any case made inevitable by the downgrading of the secret police and the public disavowals of Stalinism—meant that Khrushchev, unlike Stalin, could not achieve *both* social dynamism and the stability of his power. Stalin magnified his power as he strove to change society; to change society Khrushchev had to risk his power.[18]

The post-mobilization leader tends to be caught in a web of conflicting interests, and—lacking the coercive apparatus of his predecessors—he is likely to find himself obliged, much in the manner of a leader in a pluralist polity, to form coalitions and "pay off" others to secure acceptance and implementation of new policy departures whenever they conflict with the vested interests of competing groups and bureaucratic factions.

But whether the stability of a regime's leadership is impaired or enhanced by the abandonment of violence as a means of conflict resolution, there remains the question of the stability of the system as a whole. We have earlier seen that the coercive methods of Communist mobilization regimes tend to produce substantial alienation within the population; we would suggest

[18] Brzezinski, "The Soviet Political System: Transformation or Degeneration," p. 6.

that the higher the level of terror relative to the normative and material power used, the greater the alienation (other variables being held constant). It appears that widespread alienation is only one necessary precondition for revolutionary initiative "from below"; evidently signs of elite weakness or divided leadership are also necessary to spark the masses to protest action. Such a division within the elite may have various causes; conflict over the wisdom of using terror may well be one such cause.

The use of terror against those outside the elite can generally be rationalized by the "establishment," but its use within the elite group typically causes considerable strain among the members: it may engender insecurity; it may lead to a questioning of the normative power on which the elite is based; it may invite further violations of the group's code of behavior; it may give rise to counter-elites denouncing the use of coercion by those who had also provided the normative power on which the organization was based.[19]

To prevent or overcome such a crisis of organizational integration, the elite must strive not to dilute the power of its symbols and norms and, to this end, must safeguard a high degree of "consistency of command." By this we mean that "all commands in a system are consistent among themselves, whether they originate from a single source or from several sources."[20] Clearly an inconsistency of command may threaten the integration of the normative subsystem and in turn create conditions for a mass revolt.

Whereas in authentic post-mobilization regimes the relaxation of terror presupposes the availability of normative and material assets that may be used as functional equivalents of

---

[19] We are assuming that we are dealing here with a largely normatively integrated organization, for which as Chalmers Johnson observes "the use of force in the exercise of authority [must be] rare and carefully circumscribed." By definition, the use of terror against members of such an organization cannot normally be deemed legitimate by the other members. (See Johnson, *Revolutionary Change*, p. 31.) We do not mean to suggest that strains of guilt from terror against elite members are the only basis for normative disintegration. The norms and values that define the organization's identity and mission may, over time, show themselves to be irrelevant or incorrect reflections of reality.

[20] Deutsch, "Cracks in the Monolith," p. 310. This refers not to bureaucratic orders but to the "authoritative allocation of values."

terror, the reduction in the use of terror in derivative Communist systems need not presuppose the availability of such equivalents and—in their absence—may create the preconditions for a revolutionary situation.

In the Czech and East German riots of 1953 an alienated mass faced a more or less united elite and a loyal armed force. The "consistency of command" was successfully maintained, and the popular challenges were easily quashed, sometimes with renewed resort to violence. The situation was significantly different where crises of self-legitimation developed simultaneously within the elite: in Hungary under Imre Nagy in 1954–55; in Poland after Józef Swiatlo's defection and Gomulka's reappearance in 1954–55; in the Soviet Union after the Twentieth Congress of the CPSU in 1956. In all three instances, profound doubt and, in some cases, a sense of guilt was felt by members of the elite when the leadership was no longer able to maintain ideological unity among "captive minds" and felt obliged to denounce previously sacred symbols.[21] In 1956 the Hungarian and Polish mass revolts readily found allies and leaders within the elite. In 1968 the Czechoslovak elite opposition, in turn, found a ready and sympathetic response in the population. In these three instances, the alliance was an essential condition for successful revolution, whatever its ultimate fate.[22] In contrast, when terror was reduced in the Soviet Union, Rumania, and Yugoslavia, compensatory normative appeals either existed or were generated in time to avoid a crisis.

In the Soviet Union, the longevity of the regime itself contributed to its survival; there had been time for the routinization of behavior and the reinforcing ritualization of belief, essentially an acceptance of official norms of conduct; the bulk of the population had been successfully socialized to accept the

[21] The elite's trauma of legitimacy, aroused by doubts about terror, was further compounded by the effects of inconsistency of command on the elite's confidence in the leadership's ability to move toward the attainment of economic abundance and to maintain the integration of the party organization.

[22] This argument leans on the masterly analysis in Kecskemeti, *The Unexpected Revolution*, esp. chs. 9, 10. Inconsistency of command need not necessarily produce a revolutionary situation. The experience of Yugoslavia supports the argument that both an elite pattern and a mass pattern are needed for successful revolution.

goals of the leadership; economic hardships and political repression had been mitigated somewhat; and there existed such pacifiers as "pride in jobs well done . . . the psychic rewards of self-respect gained from altruistic behavior, the feeling of serving the common good and being approved by the Party [leadership]";[23] finally, the regime had led the country through an arduous war to national victory. In Yugoslavia, because of its role in World War II, the regime had a broad popular base that it managed to extend and strengthen as a consequence of its "hard" line vis-à-vis the Soviet Union and its "responsive" line at home after the Stalin-Tito break in 1948. Finally, in Rumania, by asserting its autonomy and courageously standing up to the Soviet Union in 1958–64, a leadership imposed on a hostile population managed to gain the legitimacy it needed to become the symbol and champion of the national cause.

Two variables thus emerge as crucial for the stability of Communist polities after the abandonment of mass terror as an instrument of national policy. Everything else (including political culture, personalities, economic constraints, external pressures and threats) being equal, there must be organization (consistency of command) and compensatory incentives (functional equivalents of terror).[24] These conditions are also crucial for economic efficiency and political institutionalization even when such extreme challenges as riots and revolts do not occur.

So far we have not dealt with the experiences of other Communist systems; in particular we have neglected China, which, like Cuba and North Vietnam, has neither completed its stage of general mobilization nor abandoned its commitment to far-

---

[23] *Ibid.*, p. 96.

[24] We advisedly leave out of consideration other dimensions of propitious revolutionary situations, since the introduction of variables not relevant to our argument would unnecessarily complicate and obscure the presentation. We have likewise chosen not to account for the varying patterns of economic conditions and demands. As for the level of development, the four countries in which riots and revolts occurred were more highly developed than Rumania, Bulgaria, and Albania. But the experience of Yugoslavia and the Soviet Union, where such outbreaks did not occur, shows that this is not by itself the decisive variable. Similarly, the role of intellectuals was considerable in Hungary, Poland, and Czechoslovakia; it was not in Rumania (where no revolt developed); but it was similarly substantial in the Soviet Union and Yugoslavia, where there was also no comparable mass pattern of revolt.

reaching transformations at home. Furthermore, even if the objective conditions for the abatement of terror were present in China, they would not be likely to be translated into a significant change of policy as long as the regime remains effectively committed to and capable of attempting attitudinal transformations, as long as it places utopian above development goals. The events of the 1960's, highlighted by the Cultural Revolution and including Mao's determination to smash the bureaucracy and coerce the intellectuals while playing down the "thought reform," may well reflect a growing disillusionment with the earlier belief in the easy remolding of human nature and a greater commitment, willy-nilly, to the use of coercive power in transforming Chinese society.

Functional Equivalents of Terror

It is a major theorem of functional analysis that "just as the same item may have multiple functions, so may the same function be diversely fulfilled by alternative items."[25] To prove the dispensability of political terror, we must show either that the functions it performs are no longer required or that there are alternatives, functional equivalents, ready to perform them. To this end, we shall briefly review the major functions of terror, as we see them, in Communist systems.

The survival and consolidation functions in operation at the takeover stage are, by definition, no longer required in the subsequent development of Communist polities.

The transformation function, too, has no operational application once the mobilization stage is passed. Presumably any future effort to carry out fundamental transformations in the society, unlikely as it seems, would require a new mobilization, under unforeseeable circumstances.

We have earlier pointed to several ancillary functions of terror. Indirectly, terror may contribute to mobilization and to the circulation of sub-elites by creating opportunities for the upward mobility of talent; it may also have normative effects,

[25] Robert Merton, *On Theoretical Sociology*, pp. 87–88.

such as deflecting the blame for failures ("scapegoatism"). At the post-mobilization stage most of these functions—to the extent that they are needed—should be able to be served adequately by other techniques. In any event, general mobilization at this stage is abandoned, by definition; terror was probably crucial to the fulfillment of only one of these functions, namely, the replacement of revolutionary cadres by younger specialists—by its very nature a nonrepetitive process.

The economic functions, forced labor, for instance, are almost incidental in the total context of coercion; served by political terror in a highly inefficient and politically costly fashion, they can be better fulfilled by other means. As for the function of atomization, the very nature of the social processes character-istic of post-mobilization development makes "atomization" no longer practicable in fact, no longer desirable in the elite's judgment, and no longer functional in theory. The natural tendency of the system is to overcome the previous elements of atomization—a tendency reinforced by demands from within the system for better information and communication.

What remains to be examined are the political control and compliance functions of terror. These can best be seen in the framework of the three processes of substitution outlined at the beginning of this chapter. The Khrushchev era provides a fine example of a many-faceted drive (resisted by bureaucratic and orthodox elements) for new "norms of legality" and due process. Whereas the courts continue to operate frequently as agencies of political coercion, the trend has been in the direction of pre-dictable and binding rules and procedures, beginning with the abolition of the Special Boards of the MVD as well as the aboli-tion of the provisions in the Criminal Code permitting sentences "by analogy."[26] Though somewhat in conflict with the tendency toward due process but typical of the Khrushchev era, experi-mentation with volunteer bodies to bring social pressure to bear

---

[26] See, for example, Harold Berman, *Justice in the USSR*; George Feifer, *Justice in Moscow*; Darrell Hammer, "Law Enforcement, Social Control and the Withering of the State"; Eugene Kamenka, "The Soviet View of Law"; and Ivo Lapenna, *Soviet Penal Policy*. For a comprehensive discussion of the legal system, see John Hazard, *Communists and Their Law*.

to secure conforming behavior provided another partial functional substitute for terror. The "people's militia" and the "comrades' courts" were examples of this effort, in part ideologically motivated and manipulated, in part intended to mobilize new resources in the struggle against deviance primarily of a nonpolitical sort, and in part intended to absolve the government and party of direct involvement and responsibility in the handling of minor misdemeanors.[27] Symptomatically, the further rationalization that came in the wake of Khrushchev's retirement led to the virtual replacement of these improvizations by regular judicial processes. At the same time, the attempts to "turn back the clock" with regard to political nonconformity have led a British student of Soviet affairs to comment that in a modern industrial society,

if it is to operate to the full extent of its capacity, contracts must be observed, political considerations must be kept within strict limits, individuals must be able to do their work in circumstances which guarantee their security as long as they fulfill their obligations to the enterprise. As compared with Stalin's era, there has been enormous improvement already in these respects. Characteristically, while in the past few years legality has sadly declined in other areas, it has remained unaffected, or has even improved, in the technical and economic spheres. But since legality is indivisible (whatever the present rulers of Soviet Russia may think) it will be necessary to extend its operation to all aspects of life without exception before there can be any certainty that it will operate reliably in the area where it is so essential to the technocrats and the planners.[28]

A second and perhaps obvious process, again best illustrated in Soviet practice, is the shift from coercive to normative power. The pervasive machinery of political persuasion, the many instrumentalities of political socialization, and the sustained efforts to inculcate official values and attitudes in the citizenry are not new. What was novel in the Khrushchev era was the effort to stage an ideological revival and to sponsor a new utopianism. After a generation of cynicism and neglect of uto-

[27] See, for example, Berman and Spindler, "Soviet Comrades' Courts"; Dennis O'Connor, "Soviet People's Guards: An Experiment with Civil Police"; Leon Lipson, "The New Face of Socialist Legality," "Socialist Legality," and "Hosts and Pests."
[28] Schapiro, "Collective Lack of Leadership," p. 200.

pian perspectives, the new era reflected both naiveté and a quest
for simpler answers, purer goals, and more glamorous targets.
Accordingly the 1961 CPSU Program terminated the "dictatorship of the proletariat" and foresaw a selective "withering" of
state institutions, although the party and its powers were to remain unchecked. As a high Soviet official explained the orientation of the moment,

> The party as an ideological-political organization depends completely
> and exclusively on persuasion of the masses; whereas the state depends
> on force as well as on persuasion. . . . The methods of persuasion . . .
> are gaining more and more ground in the life of Soviet society, and
> under Communism they will become the sole regulator of relations
> among people.[29]

In various forms and to varying degrees, education and persuasion have continued to be stressed as means of political control,
albeit in recent years with less millennial and extravagant expectations.

But, above and beyond the simple fact of a person's membership in a community, and disregarding for the moment mere
habit as well as the elements of specifically Communist education and propaganda, what would lead citizens to do voluntarily
what they had been or would otherwise have been coerced to
do? Of necessity, the answer must be impressionistic and highly
generalized. Such voluntary commitment usually has roots in
experiences or attitudes that give rise to emotions either of
pride and satisfaction—such as achievement or a shared sense
of purpose and direction—or of insecurity, whether from threats
or fear of external or internal forces. Both are apt to produce
greater identification with and reliance on the system and its
leadership.

[29] G. Shitarev, "Partiia i stroitel'stvo kommunizma," pp. 22–23. A detailed program-
matic forecast of the continual shift from coercion to persuasion, as the Soviet Union
ostensibly moves closer to full Communism, concluded that, although agencies of
coercion were still essential, "the sphere of coercion . . . is now being narrowed. . . .
Direct administrative coercion is increasingly being replaced by other forces of economic, political, and moral suasion. State coercion is getting ever closer to social coercion,
to various forms of persuasion." P. S. Romashkin, "O roli ubezhdeniia i prinuzhdeniia
v Sovetskom gosudarstve," pp. 26–29. For an analysis of the problems of coercion and
persuasion in the Khrushchev era, see Herbert Ritvo, "Totalitarianism Without Coercion?" Also, for a discussion of the relationship between coercion and pluralism, see
Douglas McCallum, "Obstacles to Change in a Communist System."

National identification is one such sentiment. One might differentiate between manipulated and spontaneous national emotions, between reactive nationalism aroused in response to external threats, as in the Soviet Union in World War II, and in Rumania and North Vietnam more recently, and authentic nationalism, which is part and parcel of the values and myths with which the regime comes to power, China being the outstanding example. Yet it is impossible to specify just how much diffuse support a regime needs, or thinks it needs, to dispense with terror. At the crucial stage of sanction substitution, numerous intervening variables may alter the outcome from case to case.

Another source of positive identification is belief in the system's effectiveness, especially when reflected in economic growth evidenced by the system's capacity to satisfy consumer demands and to raise living standards. Finally, positive identification may be produced for some groups by social and political participation. This may be true of those relatively few (except in Yugoslavia) who participate in making rules and decisions; but it may also be true of the many more citizens who are involved in ritual ratification, in various forms of implementation, and in mass organizations, or what has been labeled "participatory bureaucracy."[30] We should add that these possible forms and degrees of identification may be expected to vary considerably: things are likely to be a good deal more complex than, say, a simple correlation of regime effectiveness with regime legitimacy. In practice, positive responses may well range from tacit and routinized acquiescence in norms of social conduct on the part of those who support the system as a matter of self-interest, for example, to diffuse support based on the internalizing of the regime's values.[31]

In the 1960's Soviet authorities apparently concluded that the

[30] See Meyer, "USSR, Incorporated," pp. 369–76.
[31] Personal success in or anticipation of job satisfaction or advancement, educational opportunities, improvement of status, leisure, and creature comforts may have similar consequences, but these do not necessarily assure a more willing or eager acceptance of the regime's values. On the contrary, they may well generate "rising expectations," privatism, and a stronger quest for release from political control.

heavy reliance on "moral suasion" had been misplaced. Ideology seemed to meet with widespread skepticism. After Khrushchev's ouster most of his doctrinal innovations were ignored. The rate of economic growth slowed for a time, and vertical mobility became more restricted. Despite the continuing esoteric argument over moral vs. material incentives—both in the Soviet Union and in Communist Eastern Europe—a growing effort was made to provide more "material incentives," tangible, nonpolitical rewards in the form of additional compensation, bonuses, goods, and services for increased productivity or efficiency and for loyal, rational, and innovative performance.[32]

Although conflicting emphases in public pronouncements appeared to reflect different views among Communist officials on the preferred balance of normative, material, and coercive power, such speeches and articles would typically stress all three. Curiously, they would often include a fourth element—organization. As early as 1961 the head of the Central Committee's Department of Administrative Organs declared that in the Soviet state the "main method of governing is through persuasion, education, and organization" (adding that this "does not of course exclude the use of compulsion . . . [which] remains an important means of eradicating crime" but must be resorted to "only when all other methods have failed or when violation is particularly dangerous").[33] Similar references to organization were made even more frequently in the post-Khrushchev days. Whether or not bureaucratic organization per se creates support is a matter for further study. For our purposes, bureaucratic

[32] It should be noted that the increase in material incentives is meant to serve purposes other than those served by terror. It may nonetheless be functional in building diffuse support.

Some of the Soviet discussion regarding economic reform has been couched in terms of the tension between "administrative methods" (a euphemism for coercion) and economic considerations (i.e. material incentives). In September 1965 the Central Committee found it to be "a serious shortcoming" in economic management that "administrative methods have prevailed over economic ones" (*Pravda*, Oct. 1, 1965). And a leading Soviet economist explained that administrative methods in management "are implemented by means of the sanctions of power, that is, by extra-economic coercion." While acknowledging that coercion is at times necessary, he proceeded to argue that it is possible to shift increasingly to a "system of economic interests and material stimuli." (Ya. Kronrod, "Ekonomicheskaia reforma i nekotorye problemy politicheskoi ekonomii sotsializma," 20–21.)

[33] N. Mironov, "O sochetanii ubezhdeniia i prinuzhdeniia."

organization is best thought of as situated at the threshold of normative and coercive power, possessing characteristics of both. As an instrument of political control, organization has since Lenin's time ranked high among Communist values.[34]

The third process by which we suggest political terror may be curtailed is by reducing the assets for or the total scope of political control. Only in Yugoslavia, where terror was abandoned largely for other reasons, has this process been explicitly acknowledged, though in Czechoslovakia the shortlived changes of 1968 showed how fast and how far it can go. Yet conceptually such a retreat from totalism follows from the differentiation of state and society, from the development of greater subgroup articulation and autonomy—in short, from the gradual transition from a prescriptive to a restrictive system. But precisely because it clashes with so major and traditional an orientation, Communist elites have difficulty in acknowledging the necessity or desirability of meaningful autonomy, pluralism, or zones of depolitization.

Official prescription in certain fields, such as science, has considerably lessened in post-Stalin Russia and Eastern Europe, and close observers have identified the demand for greater "party-free spheres" as a continuing object of political dispute.[35] Kádár's formula, "He who is not against us, is with us," implies a similar zone of indifference. It is true that the Soviet regime, although it has become "less repressive," has not demonstrated any explicit willingness to become "less comprehensive."[36] But in practice the reduction in scope has more often been a result of inefficiency than political design, especially in Eastern Europe; and, even more important, the leadership finds it in-

[34] See, for example, Schapiro, *The Communist Party of the Soviet Union*; and Philip Selznick, *The Organizational Weapon*. A study of a different kind of total organization concludes that "a pattern of communication serves as a functional equivalent for force in maintaining or subverting a stable system of authority." Richard McCleery, "Policy Change in Prison Management," p. 400.

[35] Leonhard, "Politics and Ideology in the Post-Khrushchev Era," pp. 67–68. An authoritative editorial in the Warsaw *Trybuna Ludu* (Nov. 3, 1968) declared, in condemning the Dubček regime: "It is impossible to grant the slogan of 'free play of forces' in a socialist society. . . . [Yet the Dubček leadership] inclined to the concept of 'free play of forces' as a constitutional form of the socialist state."

[36] Lipson, "Law: The Function of Extra-Judicial Mechanisms," p. 165.

creasingly difficult to focus its attention on all arenas that it would like to control. It is, in fact, functional for the leadership to avoid "overloads" by waiting for incidents to draw its attention to a given arena. Thus,

maintenance of "ideological purity" in the arts—whatever that means —is rarely at the center of Party attention for long. Occasionally, owing to a juncture of political circumstances, it can briefly become so. As soon as the leaders turn away to a more pressing crisis or a more practical dilemma, officials of the second and third rank are left to cultivate political pastures of their own in the atmosphere the leaders have established. . . . That the regime may be distracted from its more intangible goals in the future as well is all the more probable in view of the continued ascendancy of economic over ideological tasks.[37]

Without terror, the costs of total enforcement are prohibitive.

How well Communist elites have learned this lesson remains to be seen. Just as the Communist system as a whole has found neither a stable equilibrium nor any clear formula of governance for the future, so the mix of incentive and sanction systems that they may use remains in flux. Moreover, even in the absence of a single dictator able to project his own idiosyncrasies onto the entire society at will, there may be strong obstacles to the rational and irreversible abandonment of terror. As we have seen, bureaucratic rigidity, traditionalism, vestiges of ideological commitment, insecurity, and the need for scapegoats, as well as overriding exogenous forces, may delay, distort, and complicate the system's adaptation to the post-mobilization stage; and in the process Communist systems may experience fits of terror, like those exemplified recently by the treatment of "revisionists" in post-Dubček Czechoslovakia, of Jews in Poland, and of intellectual nonconformists in the Soviet Union.

But the Communist experience suffices to confirm the strength of the secular trend away from political terror—above all, because of the growing pluralism and the awareness of the costs of terror. It shows, moreover, that functional equivalents can be substituted for terror without impairing the system's stability.

[37] Priscilla Johnson, *Khrushchev and the Arts: The Politics of Soviet Culture*, pp. 59–60.

7 Dynamics, Dialectics, and Dysfunction

Everybody realizes that one day his turn may come. Many live
in a state of continued fear. Fear at Rome is like a disease, an
epidemic. . . . It's enough to stare at anyone hard in the street or
in an inn to see him grow pale and go away in a hurry. Why?
because of fear . . . just fear. When fear grips a whole population
there isn't any explanation.

Ignazio Silone, Fontemara

We have seen that terror in Communist systems serves many
functions and purposes. It has numerous causes and consequences. Its scope and role, its success, and its impact have varied
with time and place. Dismissing all monistic interpretations,
then, we can look on terror as a funnel for multivariate transactions. But even if the evidence regarding its purposes and uses
is grossly incomplete and at times contradictory (indeed, the
concepts of terror, violence, and coercion, as commonly used,
are themselves somewhat ambiguous), we have found a basic
pattern of regularities that is congruent with the typical process
of development of Communist systems.

It has been observed—and it deserves restatement—that terror
is inherently ambiguous. It can be productive of compliance
or of alienation—or of both. It is both effective and self-defeating,[1] a characteristic, indeed, that obtains not only in Communist polities; terror, E. V. Walter remarks, "can destroy itself by
tearing apart the social organization necessary to maintain it."[2]
It is, writes Barrington Moore,

an essential element in the dictator's control [and yet] . . . from even
the most cold-blooded standpoint of self-interest there comes a point at
which the use of terror defeats its purposes. . . . The regime has to walk
a thin and not always easily discernible line between using too much
terror or too little. Too much can destroy the minimal framework
of regularity and legality necessary to maintain the total system upon

---

[1] Jerzy Gliksman in Friedrich, ed., *Totalitarianism*, pp. 72–73.
[2] Walter, *Terror and Resistance*, p. 342.

which the regime's power depends. Too little terror diminishes control at the center by permitting the growth of independent centers of authority within the bureaucracy.[3]

The use of terror may increase the effectiveness of a regime—but it may also produce disabling neurosis or paralysis among the citizens. It may suppress and split asunder autonomous groups in society, yet in turn it may provoke the formation of defensive coalitions. It may control deviant behavior but also may stimulate more evasion, concealment, and dissent, by the very fact of its being applied. And though it may atomize society, terror also may "serve to establish and maintain the identity and boundary lines" of oppositional groups.[4] Given a conflict of values between the leadership and society, the use of terror may prevent the regime from acquiring legitimacy but may also prevent the rise of independent forces that could effectively challenge it. Terror may both hinder socialization by alienating large segments of the population and facilitate socialization by insulating the population from competing values. Which of these effects has greater impact may well hinge on the availability of compensatory normative and material incentives. But, of course, a regime may be unwilling to release its grip to find out whether value consensus lies behind compliant behavior.

These unintended consequences defy the totalitarian leader's quest for both comprehensive control and change. Terror may stifle not only the expression of incongruent values but also "initiative, innovation, and progress."[5] Unless terror escalates, it tends to become "blunt" and, over time, may engender fatalism. But if it does escalate, its unintended consequences become all the clearer: they may include paralyzing fear, denunciations, purges, and the shirking of responsibilities, all of which sap or waste funds, resources, and skills. Meanwhile, feeding on itself,

[3] Moore, *Terror and Progress—USSR*, pp. 175–78. "Terror becomes at the same time the motor and the brake of social life." (Thierry Maulnier, *La face de Méduse du communisme*, p. 60.) See also Lifton, *Thought Reform*, pp. 237, 411; and Goffman, *Asylums*, p. 48.
[4] Lewis Coser, *The Functions of Social Conflict*, p. 38.
[5] Meyer, *The Soviet Political System*, p. 336.

the terror machine tends to grow into an empire within an empire, developing its own logic and momentum.[6] Even Carl J. Friedrich—so authoritative a voice for many years in his insistence on the key role of terror in totalitarian systems—is prepared to recognize that totalitarian terror "grows until it reaches the limit where it becomes self-defeating."[7]

Socioeconomic development in itself does not serve as a functional substitute for terror. As Karl Deutsch has pointed out, technological advances do not typically overcome a regime's lack of legitimacy; neither surveillance nor persuasion can be automated; if anything, the job of governing becomes harder, not easier, as the complexity of the system increases.[8] But development does create the preconditions for the curtailment of terror, and provides a greater fund of material and normative assets to be substituted for coercive power. It also leads ironically to a situation in which a society becomes so highly differentiated and specialized that no amount of sophisticated technology and organization can even approach total control of the citizens' behavior. At the same time, the regime knows that to abandon terror is to allow the expression of dissent, which in turn may provoke new waves of repression.[9]

This very ambiguity has given rise to widely varying assessments of the dynamics and effectiveness of terror. At one extreme is the view that the modal product of political terror is compulsive compliance. Alex Inkeles persuasively describes the dynamics of terror as a device for channeling and institutionalizing anxiety:

The regime seeks to create in every man the nagging fear that he may have done something wrong, that he may have left something undone, that he may have said some impermissible thing. It is an important part of the pattern that he be unable ever to find out exactly what it was that he did wrong. In this light the studied caprice of the terror in its impact on its actual victims may be seen in a new light. The non-

[6] Fainsod, *How Russia Is Ruled*, pp. 441, 461.
[7] Friedrich and Brzezinski, *Totalitarian Dictatorship and Autocracy*, rev. ed., p. 162.
[8] In Friedrich, ed., *Totalitarianism*, pp. 320–25.
[9] See, for example, Skilling, "Background to the Study of Opposition."

victim, looking at the actual victim, can never find out why the victim was victimized, because there are different and contradictory reasons for different victims, or there may have been no reason at all.

The non-victim thus becomes the prisoner of a vague uncertainty which nags him. It is this nagging uncertainty in the non-victim which the terror seeks to create. For it is a powerful force in making every man doubly watch his every step. It is prophylactic in the extreme. It will make the citizen properly compulsive about saying correct things in public and saying them loud for all to hear, or, almost as good, it will teach him to say nothing in public. It will wake him in the middle of the night to go back to his office to do his sums over again, to redraw his blueprint and then redraw it again, to edit and then edit again the article he is writing, to check and then recheck and then check his machine again. Anxiety demands relief, and compulsive reiteration of action is one of the most common human patterns for the handling of anxiety. It is this compulsive conformity which the totalitarian regime wants. It gets it as a derived benefit from the influence of terror on the non-victim, who puzzles over the reasons for the treatment of the victim. Anxiety has been institutionalized.[10]

But this is, and Inkeles recognizes it, only one possible pattern of adaptation. Responses to anxiety may take other forms.[11] Anxiety may produce enthusiastic behavior as a sort of protective coloration; it may engender foot-dragging, either calculated or else as a form of partial paralysis; it may stimulate a change of beliefs, attitudes, symbols of identification, or self-definition, to adapt to those promoted by the regime; and it may also generate resistance.

One way of ordering this range of possible outcomes is to conceive of the two polar positions as "functional" terror securing compliant behavior and inducing a habit of conformity supportive of the regime's efforts and adaptive for the individual; and "dysfunctional" terror, as a result of which the individual is unable to operate "normally," to orient his behavior in a calculated manner, or to cope with the stresses of his environment.

Conceptually the problem appears to be clear: "Functions are those observed characteristics which make for the adaptation or adjustment of a given system, and dysfunctions [are] those

[10] Inkeles, "The Totalitarian Mystique," pp. 106–7.
[11] See also Jesse Pitts, "Social Control." Accordingly, conforming behavior may be shot through with repressed alienation and may easily be transformed into other reactions, such as rigidity, domineering, or deviance.

observed consequences which lessen the adaptation or adjustment of the system."[12] Unfortunately, such paradigmatic generality is of little help in uncovering criteria by which to judge whether in a given instance terror is functional or not. Ultimately, whether an observer will call functional that which promotes survival, or efficacy, or other qualitative goals will depend on his values. Indeed, we might echo Robert Merton's remark that "there is no easy way to determine the optimum utilization of resources . . . partly because of ultimate disagreement over the criteria of the optimum."[13]

If, then, it is difficult to identify the boundary between functional and dysfunctional terror empirically, it is nonetheless helpful to introduce the notion of a threshold of dysfunctionality. Its significance may become clearer if we turn our attention to individual reactions to anxiety, bearing in mind that societal transactions may after all be thought of as aggregations of individual behavior.

Dynamics of Anxiety

How does terror affect the individual? Purposive terror has as its central technique the manipulation of anxiety.[14] Even if environmental as well as personal variables are likely to intervene so as to distort the symmetry of intended and actual performance or response, one may generalize about the pattern of possible outcomes for the individual concerned.

For our purposes, one significant finding of clinical and experimental psychology is that under certain conditions fear heightens an individual's motivation to perform a given task; under other conditions it interferes with his efforts. There are exceptions (and this whole field of study is relatively young), but the general proposition that emerges from a variety of cases

---

[12] Merton, *On Theoretical Sociology*, p. 106.
[13] *Ibid.*, p. 55.
[14] We speak here of terror other than the physical liquidation of victims.
We try to follow the customary distinction between fear, as the recognition of specific danger, and anxiety, as the product of tension in anticipation of danger. Fear may be functional in operating as a warning or protection, or dysfunctional in generating anxiety, depression, or aggression. The literature on anxiety, both Freudian and otherwise, is too vast and too marginal to our focus of interest to be discussed here.

and studies states that (holding constant other variables, such as personality and culture) emotional arousal including fear tends to increase or improve individual performance up to a certain threshold, beyond which the level of performance drops off significantly. Irving Janis postulates that

as emotional arousal increases . . . the heightened activation to alleviate the unpleasant emotional state will generally lead to the mobilization of resistances . . . which eventually reach a general level where they begin to increase at a greater rate than the facilitating effects of emotional arousal; beyond this critical level . . . increases in arousal will bring diminishing returns in the degree of acceptance [of the recommended behavior].[15]

The typical pattern of responses that tends to prevail for certain physiological stresses (for instance, poisoning or exposure to extreme variations in temperature) evidently also obtains for "symbolic stresses." "Living systems respond to continuously increasing stress, first, by a lag in response, then by an overcompensatory response, and finally [beyond a putative threshold] by catastrophic collapse."[16] Studies of behavior under disaster conditions have confirmed this basic pattern, showing that "extreme stress always worsens performance, but moderate stress can improve it above ordinary levels."[17]

---

[15] Irving Janis, "Effects of Fear Arousal on Attitude Change," p. 186. Janis confirms other findings indicating that "at very high levels of emotional arousal, the average person's perceptual and cognitive functions become severely impaired," particularly when severe threats of pain or punishment are involved. (See also R. S. Lazarus et al., "The Effects of Psychological Stress upon Performance," *Psychological Bulletin*, XLIX: 4 [1952], which also reviews other experiments in this area.) Other studies have found evidence of mental regression under intense anxiety (e.g., Lazarus, *Psychological Stress*, p. 303; Whitaker and Malone, "Anxiety and Psychotherapy," pp. 167–69).

[16] "While extreme stress always worsens performance, moderate stress can improve it above ordinary levels." (J. G. Miller, "Toward a General Theory for the Behavioral Sciences," pp. 527–28.) See also Hans Selye, *The Stress of Life*, pp. 30–32, 86–87.

[17] S. B. Withey, "Reaction to Uncertain Threat," p. 104. Lazarus et al., "The Effects of Psychological Stress," p. 311, corroborate the conclusion that "in some instances high degrees of motivation or fear seem to produce a decrement or impairment of performance. . . . It is possible to think of a critical point in the amount of fear, beyond which disruption occurs."

The evidence in Janis and other studies also suggests that shame and guilt function essentially in the same fashion as fear. It might therefore be suggested hypothetically that they might constitute functional equivalents susceptible to the same manipulation as terror. (Lucian Pye, in *The Spirit of Chinese Politics*, argues that in Chinese culture shame may be manipulated for social mobilization.) An additional problem arises from conflicting but simultaneous threats—e.g., threats of physical harm and shame. It has been suggested that at lower levels of intensity, shame-anxiety may facilitate performance, while harm-anxiety may disrupt it. (Withey, "Reaction to Uncertain Threat," p. 103.) See also E. E. Levitt, *The Psychology of Anxiety*, ch. 7.

Experimental results also suggest that the greatest significant drop in performance under extreme stress occurs in the most sophisticated and complex jobs in which greater judgment and reflection are required.[18] It is understandable that in social situations where mistakes may be interpreted as acts of sabotage, those with more complex assignments should be most anxious. Beyond a certain point, then, terror becomes especially dysfunctional in a modern society where creativity and innovation, sober judgment and applied intelligence are particularly needed.

Thus we are led to hypothesize that there is a pattern, similar to that of individual responses, applicable to entire societies, where within certain limits of intensity (holding constant other variables, such as personality differences) the stimulation of anxiety tends to heighten the likelihood of compliance, but beyond which an increase in anxiety is likely to impede performance partially or completely.[19] Experimental evidence is still too contradictory and incomplete to allow a clear distinction between the effect of anxiety on behavior change and on attitude change. Here, however, we are helped by Festinger's work in the field of cognitive dissonance, in which the concept of "forced compliance" seems substantially similar to our notion of the deprivation of alternatives.[20] Forced compliance, by which is meant compliant public behavior without an accompanying change in private attitudes or beliefs, according to Festinger, can be brought about by threats of punishment (i.e. coercive power) or special reward (i.e. normative or material power). Assuming an inherent striving toward consistency of attitude and behavior, the consequence for the individual of such inconsist-

[18] Levitt, p. 152.

[19] An additional hypothesis regarding the effects of terror is suggested by the finding that after intense personal disaster, taboos on the public recall of the circumstances of traumatic experiences lead to prolonged emotional difficulties, and the fear of recurrences of the disaster is nourished by the memory of the original experience. (D. W. Chapman, "Dimensions of Models in Disaster Behavior," p. 324.) In this light Khrushchev's "secret" speech may be taken to have performed an unwittingly therapeutic role in breaking the taboo and facilitating the abandonment of diffuse anxiety about the recurrence of terror.

[20] This is what Brzezinski has labeled the "dilemma of the only alternative" in totalitarian systems. Walter (*Terror and Resistance*, pp. 286–89) speaks of it as "forced choice"—in his approach, a distinct phenomenon, complementary to terror. Harold Lasswell correctly suggests that the notion of coercion implies the absence of choice (*Psychopathology and Politics*, p. 277).

ency is cognitive dissonance, which is found to be a motivating force of its own. To reduce the dissonance, an individual may seek to alter either his attitude or his behavior; and the likelihood of such an adjustment being made is greater the greater the dissonance. (Dissonance in turn is found to be a weighted function of the perceived importance of the opinion contradicted by overt behavior and of the perceived magnitude of the threat or reward.)

There is considerable experimental evidence to support the view that the pressures to seek consonance are greatest when the dissonant elements are of roughly equal proportion—that is, if the threat is not so overwhelming as to dwarf the relative importance to the individual of maintaining personal consonance. It follows that

if one wanted to obtain private change in addition to mere public compliance, the best way to do this would be to offer just enough reward or punishment to elicit the overt compliance. If the reward or threat were too strong, only little dissonance would be created and one would not expect private change to follow as often.[21]

Thus, when the perceived intensity of terror compared to the behavior assumed to be required to avoid punishment is overwhelming, there is little psychic pressure to adjust attitudes and beliefs to outward acts so as to restore consonance.

If then there is scientific support for the generalization that mild terror tends to be more effective in optimizing performance than extreme terror, it follows that once terror diminishes, the pressure within the individual to bring his views and his be-

[21] Leon Festinger, *A Theory of Cognitive Dissonance*, p. 95. See also J. W. Brehm and A. R. Cohen, *Explorations in Cognitive Dissonance*, which cites additional examples to show that "severe threat is a cognition more consistent with giving up a desirable object than is a mild threat. Thus the subjects in the mild threat condition would experience greater dissonance" and would therefore be more likely to change attitudes (pp. 41–42). It also confirms that "dissonance increases as the magnitude of the coercive force to comply decreases" (pp. 85–88). On the other hand, it introduces the additional complicating variable of volition, which the authors suggest varies inversely with coercive force and may therefore operate in the opposite direction of Festinger's paradigm (pp. 201–10). The problem appears to be still too unexplored to draw more general conclusions, especially with regard to sociopolitical phenomena. See also Withey, "Reaction to Uncertain Threat," pp. 118–19; and, more generally, Lazarus, *Psychological Stress*; C. A. Insko et al., "Effects of High and Low Fear-Arousing Communication upon Opinion"; and N. Leventhal et al., "The Effects of Fear . . . upon Attitudes and Behavior."

havior into consonance is likely to increase. In a political setting
such adjustment may result either in a change in attitudes, producing greater legitimacy for the regime, or in a change in
behavior, producing greater manifest dissent or deviance. Surely
the experience of the post-mobilization stage in the Soviet
Union and Eastern Europe tends to bear out this hypothesis,
for the reduction of political terror has both strengthened the
legitimacy of Communist regimes and significantly increased
the total of overt dissent.

Terror and Totalitarianism

We have seen that although terror may fulfill other functions
as well, its two core functions during a Communist system's stage
of general mobilization are control and change—precisely the
the central tendencies in Communist development as a whole.[22]
Insofar as it is used rationally, in other words, political terror
is one of the essential instrumentalities at the service of the
system. In this light, one may indeed say[23] that terror is the
"linchpin" of totalitarian systems, though not necessarily of all
Communist regimes.

We earlier defined our use of the term, totalitarianism, in
regard to Communist systems by equating it with their mobilization stage. Lest we be charged with dismissing the very real
problem of the relationship between totalitarianism and terror
by arbitrary definitional legerdemain, let us now consider it in
the light of typical performance characteristics of totalitarian
systems. As an ideal type, a totalitarian system involves the
commitment of all resources required for the attainment of an

[22] See above, p. 6.

[23] As Fainsod did (*How Russia Is Ruled*, 1st ed. [1953], p. 354). It is interesting to
note the Nazi analysis of this problem: "Fear is the cheapest but also the least reasonable
method of securing allegiance which, in unavoidable military and political crises, will
fail soonest and turn into its opposite. . . . If the method is not used in the right proportions, the danger exists . . . that despair and hatred will make the oppressed an un-
inhibited and fanatical active enemy. . . . Fear in the form of a shock effect may also
serve to bridge over an especially critical span of time during which it prevents the
intimidated population from rendering support to the enemy or attempting an open
uprising. However, it must be remembered that every such shock remains effective only
a limited time and then produces an even more violent reaction of bitterness and hatred."
(SS Colonel von Loew, at a German state security staff conference, June 8, 1944; cited
in W. H. Kraus and G. A. Almond, "Resistance and Repression Under the Nazis,"
pp. 46–47.)

overriding goal. In Communist systems this means a monopoly of ideology and organization by the ruling elite, as well as its control of all relevant assets—organized force, economy, communications, arts, and science. Hence, all human endeavor becomes politicized, all human relationships are subjected to planning and organization, and all values and demands are subordinated to the dominant goal.[24] To achieve this, the ruling elite or its leader must use coercion to overcome resistance, opposition, evasion, and inertia. Thus, the use of force or the credible threat of its use is bound to be involved in the achievement of totalitarian controls, their maintenance, and their use to transform society, economy, and man.

It follows, then, that "the term 'totalitarian'. . . implies coercion or repression."[25] It cannot be proven that such coercion must necessarily take the form of terror, but it is difficult to imagine a system of calculable coercion operating effectively under such pressures. (Besides, terror has the advantage of economy, for it does double duty: its application typically both disposes of its victims and "terrorizes" untold others, to a degree that calculable coercion could not.)

The experience to date shows that all Communist polities have sooner or later moved to maximize central control and to embark on the general mobilization of society. One may conceive of Communist regimes that in the future would be content to operate without seeking such "total" control or without sweeping development and transformation goals, but clearly this would extend the connation of "Communism" to a new and different phenomenon. The record also shows that, all other variables assumed constant, the greater the speed or the magnitude of the attempted transformation, the more extensive or intensive the terror required.

We have seen that the actual use of terror in any given

---

[24] See Meyer, *The Soviet Political System*, pp. 471–72; Neumann, *The Democratic and the Authoritarian State*, pp. 244–45.

[25] Moore, *Political Power and Social Theory*, p. 31. See also Friedrich and Brzezinski, *Totalitarian Dictatorship*, ch. 13; Fainsod, *How Russia Is Ruled*, 1st ed., p. 354, and rev. ed., pp. 421–22.

instance is affected by a variety of other considerations, one of which is the availability of alternative assets. Typically, the paucity of material resources available for use as incentives and the weakness of normative support make for a correspondingly greater requirement of coercive power. Although the transformation of the system both to achieve "total" control and to use it requires substantial coercion, the maintenance of such a system of effective political control does not normally demand a great expenditure of power. This distinction appears to be congruent with the dichotomy between a prescriptive and a restrictive system: transformation requires prescription of behavior patterns, and greater coercion, whereas mere control requires only restriction of deviance within certain bounds of the tolerable. A restrictive system, then, may be indicated for a regime that has in effect eschewed sweeping societal transformation goals, such as Communist systems beyond the stage of general mobilization.

One of the tragic illusions of Communist leaders is their hubris—the Promethean belief in their ability to reshape men and societies at will, coupled with faith in the unlimited perfectibility of man and society—an outlook reinforced by their dictatorial powers but seemingly unaffected by the irrepressible consequences of their own actions. In practice, a totally prescriptive system is an impossibility. No regime has the means to dictate effectively and check on the political, economic, and social behavior of all its citizens. Nevertheless, at the mobilization stage Communist regimes come closer to this utopian prospect than any others. Such a system, characterized by an incongruence between ends and means and by the use of varying degrees of coercion for the control of all three types of behavior, is able to rely extensively on the demonstration effects of terror to deter potential deviance in all sectors of society.[26] Though it may be

---

[26] We assume that to a limited extent it is always possible to substitute one form of power for another, though (1) some minimal investment of each of the three types of power—coercive, normative, and material—is needed at all times, and (2) there are different degrees of "fit" between such power mixes and the different kinds of goals.

effective, such a strategy is markedly inefficient; in the long run, material incentives are far more conducive to economic performance than is terror. Terror is also inefficient because it causes widespread alienation.[27] Yet given the urgency that Communist systems attach to the tasks of transformation, and given the lack of adequate material and normative assets, the reliance on terror in its rational aspects is an effective element in their strategy of "primitive accumulation."

Once the mobilization process has successfully passed a critical point, however, the regime is confronted with the need to make new and difficult choices. Pressures abound for the abatement of terror and a recognition of the impossibility of continuing to strive for total prescription of behavior. Criteria of efficiency now tend to replace effectiveness as the standards of evaluation of performance. And a strain toward congruence of means and ends becomes operative. Thus, diffuse terror tends to disappear, giving way to the application of coercion primarily for the purpose of controlling deviance beyond certain limits of official tolerance; that is, a restrictive strategy is employed to cope with dissent. At the same time, economic behavior tends to be increasingly manipulated by material incentives. Finally, ideology gradually turns into a stable value system (to use Chalmers Johnson's terminology), becoming a source of normative power for long-term socialization.

In short, the legacy of the mobilization stage—with its complex strategy of prescription, effectiveness, and incongruence, and with the central role that terror plays in this strategy—

As Etzioni has persuasively shown (in his *The Active Society*, pp. 370–72 and *passim*), there is a congruence between goals pursued and assets used when cultural goals are implemented with normative power, production goals with material power, and order goals with coercive power. To avoid semantic confusion, it should be pointed out that where Etzioni speaks of "utilitarian power" we refer to "material power"; and whereas Etzioni describes a state of congruence as one of "effectiveness," we refer to congruence as efficient, and to incongruence as effective, though wasteful.

[27] It is our impression that, after the initial elimination of political opponents of the revolutionary regime, terror has tended to alienate the population primarily from the regime and the representatives of authority, rather than from community values; this seems to be increasingly true as more compensatory (normative and material) values become available. A comparative study of the various facets of alienation and support in Communist systems remains to be undertaken.

shapes the way in which the dominant problems are handled in the post-mobilization stage, with a typical pattern of restriction, efficiency, and congruence, and a diminishing tolerance of terror, as the regime is obliged to take cognizance of multiple goals and multiple interests in its society.

Strength and Stability

One of the questions that has sharply divided interpreters of Communist policy concerns the typical preconditions for terror campaigns (presumably, as perceived by the decision-makers). Are they launched from relative strength or weakness? One school of thought argues that terror increases as opposition (i.e. the "objective" need for terror) decreases.[28] Another maintains that "the widespread and habitual use of terror is an admission of insecurity, weakness, and lack of legitimacy."[29]

The second interpretation accords with the Leninist rationale for terror, namely, that it was resorted to only when a severe danger loomed and that it was again curtailed—or should have been—when the situation improved. As an authoritative Soviet account put it in the 1920's: "The scope of proletarian terror was always congruent with the political circumstances of the moment, reaching its maximal intensity and acuity at the moments of bitterest struggle and then dropping back to a mini-

---

[28] Arendt, *The Origins of Totalitarianism*, p. 91. This assertion, that "terror increases . . . in inverse ratio to the existence of internal political opposition" (p. 91), may be contradicted, it is true, by the same author's statement that terror—"the essence of totalitarian domination"—"becomes total when it becomes independent of all opposition" (p. 162), and even more by her assertion that "impotence breeds violence" and "every decrease of power is an open invitation to violence." (Arendt, "Reflections on Violence," pp. 20, 35.)

Brzezinski posits the need for a totalitarian leader to assure both loyalty and dynamism and sees terror as a means of disposing of the complacent, the failures, and the inefficient, something the system can best afford to do at times of relative stability (*The Permanent Purge*, pp. 18, 27). He also points to the examples of Poland and East Germany during the final years of Stalin to show that the weakness of their regimes justified evading Soviet orders, i.e., permitted them plausibly to insist that they were too weak to stage purge trials. (*The Soviet Bloc*, p. 97, see also p. 91; Friedrich and Brzezinski, *Totalitarian Dictatorship*, 1st ed., pp. 150, 155; and Gundersheim, "Terror and Political Control," pp. 13–14, who argues that in Nazi Germany and the Soviet Union "the opposition was not the pretext for the terror but the last impediment to its full realization.") Calvert argues that terror is used by governments that lack legitimacy but that the more ineffective the opposition the more likely "an orgy of coercion to establish [the regime's] will." (N. P. Calvert, "Revolution: The Politics of Violence," p. 10.)

[29] Meyer, *The Soviet Political System*, p. 336.

mum, to the extent that the dictatorship of the proletariat gained in stability."[30] This is also the underlying assumption of Khrushchev's argument in his "secret" speech:

> Lenin used severe methods only in the most necessary cases, when the exploiting classes were ... vigorously opposing the Revolution, when the struggle for survival was decidedly assuming the sharpest forms. ... Stalin, on the other hand, used extreme methods and mass repressions at a time when the Revolution was already victorious, when the Soviet state was [stabilized], when the exploiting classes were already liquidated and socialist relations were rooted solidly in all phases of national economy, when our party was politically consolidated and had strengthened itself both numerically and ideologically.[31]

Khrushchev implies that Stalin acted either irrationally or out of a calculus that permitted him to risk the disruptive concomitants of terror during periods of relative stability or availability of what he perceived to be compensating normative power.

We do not know, of course, how realistically Communist leaders perceive domestic and foreign threats, but we do find that a comparison of the experience of various Communist countries reveals a clear pattern: especially among "derivative" regimes, those that found their society in a condition of relative stability and cohesion on the eve of terror (Hungary and Czechoslovakia) were willing and presumably able to use more terror at the mobilization stage than those that did not. Conversely, those that suffered from social and political instability (Poland, East Germany, perhaps North Korea) were among the states that—presumably out of fear of the alienating consequences—used the least terror in the extension of political control and in agricultural transformation at the mobilization stage.

If then we review the two positions—terror from weakness or from strength—let us submit that both apply. Stability requires less terror for control but allows more terror for change. One may well think of political terror as intended to bridge the gap between middle-range goals and available means, and the mag-

---

[30] "Terror," in *Entsiklopediia gosudarstva i prava*, III, 1170. See also above, ch. 2, n. 10.

[31] *The Anti-Stalin Campaign and International Communism*, pp. 18–19.

nitude of terror required as roughly proportionate to the magnitude of the gap, under conditions of relative scarcity of normative and material assets. In other words, to the extent that it is used rationally, political terror may be resorted to when the government has no other adequate means or no other means it is willing to use to assure political stability or compliance with its directives; or else it may be employed for the attainment of particularly costly or onerous transformations—in social stratification, in economic organization, or in behavior patterns, for example. Typically, such transformations will be timed or paced so as not to overstrain the system, by a strategy giving rise to alternations of rapid transformation and retrenchment. As we have seen, attempts at simultaneous transformations impose geometrically higher costs in stress, terror, and dislocation. In this context, the width of the gap between means and ends may be but need not be a measure of weakness; it may also be the result of various pressures on the policy-makers, and/or the product of a rational strategy: the quantum of terror employed cannot be taken as an indicator of the relative weakness of the regime. The phenomenon is, after all, a familiar one. A certain moderate expenditure of fuel is required for the ordinary operation of a motor vehicle, whereas a drive uphill or over difficult terrain demands an additional quantity of fuel. Similarly, the number of calories burned up by the human body in extra exertion provides a parallel to the greater need for coercive power for transformation campaigns.

Terror may then be used, for different purposes, under conditions of either weakness or strength.[32] In either case it serves as a political boost from the world of the desired to the realm of reality. Any study of the elements of strength and weakness that condition this boost must explore the extent to which terror

[32] The options open to the regime in this regard are analogous to those familiar to students of Soviet foreign policy. In the Comintern days, for instance, the use of foreign Communist parties as a tool of Soviet policy, in pursuit of a militant strategy of "direct action" was appropriate both during phases of especial Soviet weakness, when the parties abroad could serve as border guards (in Trotsky's phrase) of the Soviet state by making trouble in the potential enemy's rear (e.g., in 1928–33), and during periods of optimism concerning early revolutionary opportunities abroad (e.g., in 1919, 1921, and 1923). In the former case, it was essentially a matter of survival and maintenance; in the latter, of transformation.

campaigns are planned in advance. Foreign observers have often
been inclined to endow Communist policy-makers with uncanny
skill in social engineering—partly out of ignorance of Communist decision-making processes, partly because of Communist
claims to uniquely "scientific" insights. Actually, without in
any way denying the general rationality of means we have elsewhere posited, it is well to bear in mind some alternative perspectives. In the East European states, for a number of years
the general strategy of terror was imposed in blanket fashion
from outside, without particular concern about its applicability
to local conditions. In other countries, such as China, the re-
versals and zigzags of policy have been sufficiently publicized
and violent to leave little doubt of the trial-and-error nature of
policy sequences. In the Soviet Union under Stalin the use of
terror was frequently escalated by those who had a vested interest in its success, at times confronting top policy-makers with
a virtual fait accompli; the same was evidently true in Hungary
and Czechoslovakia in 1949–52. But even when this was not the
case, it seems that decisions were basically incremental. Thus,
as we saw above, Stalin's primary decision on collectivization
was largely improvised and, once being implemented, "logically" led to further and harder decisions, with little elbow
room short of retreat—typically, Stalin would not retreat. Similarly, in the Great Purge, Stalin at the time of the Kirov assassination in 1934 "may not have made his motives explicit even
to himself. One fatal error led to another and forced him to pay
a higher price for his security than he originally expected."[33]

One must therefore conclude that terror has not been wielded
as a precision tool by those who exercise the art of government
in Communist polities. This is generally true of other systems
as well.[34] In Communist systems, in particular, the imperfections
of information feedback are severe; and the arbitrary, stubborn

[33] *The Economist* (London), Oct. 19, 1968. See also Rigby, *Communist Party Membership*, pp. 213ff. For a persuasive presentation of a similar process in China, see
Michel Oksenberg, "Policy Formulation in Communist China: The Case of the Mass
Irrigation Campaign, 1957–58."
[34] See D. A. Neubauer and L. D. Kastner, "The Study of Compliance Maintenance
as a Strategy for Comparative Research."

one-man decisions of a Stalin or Rákosi add to the problem, making terror campaigns in practice far more a chain of minor decisions than an implementation of a clear, clean, and careful design.

As with the preconditions of terror, there is disagreement over stability vs. instability as outcomes of its use. Some analysts seem to confuse destabilization as an objective consequence and as an intended condition, and others fail to specify whether societal or individual destabilization is at stake. But the problem is highlighted by Barrington Moore in his stress on the self-defeating nature of terror, the fact that it "ultimately destroys the network of stable expectations concerning what other people will do that lie at the core of any set of organized human relationships."[35] This version, with which we concur, carries no necessary assumption of intent on the part of Communist leaders, nor even of their awareness of the process.

It is a different thing to claim that totalitarianism requires institutionalized "terror of permanent instability," or to insist that mass atomization must mean destabilization for the individual citizen.[36] Perhaps the most persuasive formulation of this perspective is Merle Fainsod's conclusion that "the insecurity of the masses must be supplemented by the insecurity of the governing elite who surround the dictator."[37] There can be no doubt that by its very nature the unpredictability of terror makes for a destabilization of individual expectations. Nor is there any ground for questioning the purposive disruption of traditional behavior patterns, which, as we have seen in the Soviet case, is operationally an end in itself and in the Chinese

[35] Moore, *Terror and Progress—USSR*, p. 176. It is true that elsewhere Moore refers to the "vested interest in confusion" as an "essential element in the internal dynamics of totalitarianism" (*Political Power and Social Theory*, p. 20).

[36] Arendt, *Totalitarianism*, pp. xv, xvi, 21. Kornhauser argues in a related vein that "totalitarianism is limited only by the need to keep large numbers of people in a state of constant activity controlled by the elite" (*The Politics of Mass Society*, p. 123).

[37] Fainsod, *How Russia Is Ruled*, rev. ed., p. 441. Neumann (*The Democratic and the Authoritarian State*, pp. 275–93) may well have attributed too much subtlety to totalitarian leaders in suggesting that they create neurotic anxiety among their followers "to tie the led so closely to the leader that they would perish without identification with him." This also does not explain the phenomenon in respect to those who do not regard themselves as willing followers.

case, at least in conception, is a prelude to reintegration along new lines. Clearly, to a Communist policy-maker "destabilization" must seem preferable to hostile behavior or attitudes, whereas reintegration into patterns of officially sponsored values is preferable to "destabilization" (just as in international relations neutrality is preferable to membership in a hostile alliance system, but alignment with the Communist camp is preferable to neutrality).

But ultimately the rulers must recognize that societal destabilization cannot be a foundation for permanence, let alone efficiency. As Gundersheim, among others, has argued, Communist societies too need a degree of order and stability to bring about the basic social, economic, and political changes to which the ruling elite is committed. Some Chinese leaders, though apparently not Mao, have well learned the disruptive consequences of the Great Leap and the Cultural Revolution. Thus, while seeking to assure their domination and the suppression of dissent, and while instituting dynamic changes, the leadership is typically intent on circumscribing the anxiety and instability that its own actions are bound to engender; in other words, "the means used to attain the desired ends must not vitiate the possibility of attaining those ends."[38] Moreover, the successful maintenance of the control system requires the image of regime stability that might otherwise be easily jeopardized, given repressed doubts and anxiety in the population. "Under conditions of social instability, these doubts become conscious, active sources of disloyalty."[39] Terror, in other words, must not be allowed to cross the threshold of dysfunctionality.

True, this may be giving the policy-makers too much credit: making the attainment of their long-range ends impossible would appear to be typical of the "unintended consequences" of their own actions or of the mutual incompatibility of their objectives. It is also questionable whether the leaders recognize the stresses for the system stemming from personal disorienta-

[38] Gundersheim, "Terror and Political Control," pp. 86, 93–94.
[39] Inkeles and Bauer, *The Soviet Citizen*, pp. 290–91.

tion and destabilization. It does indeed appear that Stalin, like other dictators, derived personal comfort from the discomfort of his subordinates, whom he contrived to keep at loggerheads with each other, as Khrushchev later revealed. It is at this point that the intervening impact of individual leaders becomes critical. Given the tendency of highly bureaucratized systems to frustrate minute control from the center, a leader has a variety of options open to him, from giving up his desire for total control to finding means to circumvent bureaucratization, from terroristic purges to instituting overlapping bureaucratic jurisdictions. This suggests that in the mobilization stage Communist polities tend to exhibit a functional bias toward systemic destabilization; how the leadership copes with it needs to be seen from case to case. In the post-mobilization stage, however, operationally dropping or neglecting the goal of total control means the end of this "functional bias": here is a prime example of the interaction between volitional and determinist elements.

What might well be granted on the basis of the few cases to date is a strong component of ambivalence in the attitude of Communist elites, based on a conflict between two desirable but incompatible values. Once again this hypothesis may be supported by analogy with Communist ambivalence or disagreement in other areas of political and military affairs—fundamentally, the cleavage between the "leftist" advocates of "the worse, the better"—a destabilizing strategy—and the "rightist" impulse toward stabilization through law and order and central control. Characteristically, as Richard Lowenthal points out, this does indeed correspond to the difference between Soviet and Chinese strategies. Although personality and cultural differences may be responsible for this cleavage as well, variations in the more manifest degree of optimism regarding the future and of commitment to the manipulation of the environment would seem to point to the roots of two fundamentally unreconciled approaches within Communism.

8 The Balance of Terror

But our shudders are all for the "horrors" of the minor Terror,
the momentary Terror, so to speak; whereas, what is the horror of
swift death by the axe compared with lifelong death from hunger,
cold, insult, cruelty, and heartbreak? What is swift death by
lightning compared with death by slow fire at the stake?

Mark Twain

Political terror is generally effective in making possible the
attainment of immediate goals—the liquidation of real, potential, or imaginary rivals for power and authority; the elimination or isolation of those suspected of actually or potentially
holding beliefs and attitudes at variance with the official ones—
as well as the next higher level of goals that terror campaigns
are intended to serve, such as the collectivization of agriculture.
If these were the only criteria for assessing the effectiveness of
terror, it would have to be adjudged an overwhelming success. But what of the middle-range objectives that terror is sup-
posed to subserve and the costs and unintended consequences
of terror?

Effectiveness and Efficiency

We have seen that the successful operation of the system, and
its economic development in particular, generates new tensions,
new social forces and alignments, new sources of deviance and
dissent. Communist systems have generally been unsuccessful
in sealing off their societies, and especially their elites, from
the outside world and in "freezing" them in a state of total
compliance. Ironically, both the dynamics of successful development and the stagnation of failure will tend to destabilize what
passes for total control.

More particularly, both major strategic orientations—the Stalinist concern with behavioral compliance and the Maoist con-

cern with "thought reform"—have proved to have severe short-comings from the regime's point of view. The Stalinist emphasis on compliance allowed, or rather could not prevent, mental reservations and hidden dissent on a scale incalculable by the regime; the process of securing total compliance could never be complete, and therefore there remained the need for what Franz Neumann called the "permanent threat against the individual": terror. The Chinese Communist program of thought reform sought to cope with, rather than to deny, the "contradictions" by reforming attitudes and values, an effort that, though not a total failure perhaps, surely cannot be pronounced a success, if one may judge by the attitudes exhibited during the Hundred Flowers interlude, in the setbacks of the Great Leap Forward, and in the civil strife of the Cultural Revolution.[1]

Yet terror seems to be effective not only in achieving its immediate negative (deterrent, prophylactic, or punitive) objectives, but also in securing positive behavioral compliance.[2] Here again the application of terror builds on a more general trait of "mobilized" Communist systems, the deprivation of choice. This after all is what a "prescriptive" system means, the only alterna-

[1] We can only surmise the magnitude of irrational elements, but we believe it to be generally true, as Barrington Moore discovered, that in the view of Communist leaders, terror is "a rational device to be used 'scientifically.' . . . Aside from individual instances, there is very little cruelty merely for the sake of cruelty in Soviet terror. The categories of victims are worked out by a crude but nevertheless rational procedure." (Moore, *Terror and Progress—USSR*, p. 157.) See also Beck and Godin, *Russian Purge and the Extraction of Confession*, pp. 74, 85, 229.
At the same time, there are obviously instances in which the goals appear non-sensical, unjust, impulsive, paranoid, or totally disproportionate to the occasion. But, be it the exiling of entire Soviet nationalities suspected of disloyalty, or the decimation of the cadres of party veterans in the 1930's, or of former members of the International Brigade in Spain, or the purge of a Nikolai Voznesensky or a Rudolf Slánský, terror does achieve the goals presumably set at the center.
Other elements of irrationality include the escalation of terror by zealous or self-serving security personnel and lower-level officials; instances of what appear to have been communications failures (e.g., misinterpreting or "anticipating" Stalin's wishes); and, at least in the case of Hungary, the impression that "the personal jealousies, ambitions and enmities of AVH [Hungarian secret police] and Party officials played a greater part in motivating action against particular individuals than the compromising data in their dossiers." (Ignotus, "The AVH: Symbol of Terror," p. 23.) See also Helmut Wagner, "Die Rolle des Terrors und des Persönlichkeitskultes in der Sowjetunion," p. 760.
[2] An exception concerns the instances in which an attempt is made not merely to liquidate or silence an individual but by terror to secure his active cooperation, for example to testify—sometimes in open court—against others or to admit publicly to false charges. Clearly, recalcitrance or the ability to withstand a variety of pressures and threats varies greatly with the individual involved.

tive to compliance being refusal, with the inevitable risk of personally fatal consequences.

But even if compliance, in this narrow and immediate sense, "works," what long-range alternative is there to the prospect of continual, sempiternal coercion? On the gamut from coerced compliance to enthusiastic support there are intermediate positions of unconscious adaptation that deserve closer study. People in an environment of diffuse terror learn instinctively what one may say or do and what it is safer to avoid. Such a response is functional for the individual's survival, though it by no means assures it. But even if he escapes outwardly unscathed, there are personal and social costs involved. As Bauer and Inkeles have stressed, information flow is curtailed by self-inhibition; most interpersonal ties tend to be severed or avoided; and the individual is likely to operate in a potentially self-destructive context of exaggerated assumptions regarding the omnipotence and omnipresence of the secret police or its informers. The best that the regime can hope to achieve in this way is some form of accommodation well short of normative commitment to the system but reflecting, at least in periods of relative stability, a general acceptance of existing authority.[3] Yet so long as the goals of general mobilization remain alive, such a compromise cannot be satisfactory to the rulers, because under its terms the individual may strive to avoid involvement with the political system, to depoliticize his existence, as if operating by the formula, *Non cogito ergo sum.*

Everything considered, we find that the incidence of outright commitment and full-fledged support produced by terror is

---

[3] Inkeles and Bauer, *The Soviet Citizen*, pp. 282–91. We believe that they exaggerate the extent to which such behavior is modal. However, it is certainly a widespread experience that, "realizing that any expression of doubt, disloyalty, or unreliability would prejudice his occupational chances, [the citizen of a Communist state] shuns thinking of political and other dangerous matters, learns to control the correct forms, and adheres to them."

Although it has become conventional wisdom to assert that terror leads to a withdrawal from politics, one may also argue the opposite, namely, that political terror increases mass political sensitivity. As one first-hand account claims, "Every Soviet citizen has to know at any given moment exactly what can be said and what cannot be said without coming into collision with the continually shifting Party line. This in itself has contributed substantially to the political maturity of the Russian masses." (Beck and Godin, *Russian Purge*, p. 276.)

rather low. How and when, in fact, does terror generate normative effects? One may briefly categorize such situations as follows:

(1) the Stalin assumption, i.e., a habit-forming sequence of compliances with specific orders, creating a self-reinforcing behavior pattern in the absence of viable alternatives; cognitive dissonance requires an adjustment, which may take the form of a shift of values to conform with compliant behavior;[4]

(2) support tendered by groups other than the victims, either out of complicity and a sense of guilt (the "Stavrogin phenomenon");[5] or out of a perception of a common enemy identified with the victims, either domestic or foreign, or both;[6]

(3) ready commitment congruent with certain personality types; this is a variant of what Erich Fromm labeled "escape from freedom," in which insecurity (whatever the psychoanalytic elements) makes for eager acceptance of a highly structured command system.[7] But of all forms of coercion, terror is

---

[4] Such instances are presumably most frequent under conditions of total "milieu control." It was a prison experience that a respondent related to Lifton (*Thought Reform*, p. 31): "You begin to believe all this [what you are made to say], but it's a special kind of belief. You are not absolutely convinced, but you accept it—in order to avoid trouble—because every time you don't agree, trouble starts again."

[5] Neumann (*The Democratic and the Authoritarian State*, pp. 292–93) cites as examples the SS approach, as well as the medieval Fehme murders and Dostoyevsky's *The Possessed*, to argue that the repression of guilt can be overcome only through unconditional surrender to the leader. As Stavrogin, in *The Possessed* (p. 361), declares, "Persuade four members of the circle to do in a fifth on the pretense that he is a traitor, and you'll tie them all together with the blood they've shed as though it were a knot. They'll be your slaves."

[6] The mobilization aspect of terror against real or imagined domestic enemies is the counterpart of efforts to rally the population to revolutionary movements against external enemies or threats. Typically, the official myths will allege a link between domestic and foreign "conspirators." But, as in the case of the Chinese land reform, the common domestic "enemy" may be an entirely adequate object.

[7] Paul Tillich reminisced about the mood in Germany on the eve of Hitler's takeover: "First of all a feeling of fear or, more exactly, of indefinite anxiety was prevailing. . . . A catastrophic breakdown was expected any moment. Consequently, a longing for security was growing in everybody. A freedom that leads to fear and anxiety has lost its value; better authority with security than freedom with fear." (Cited in Rollo May, "Centrality of the Problem of Anxiety in Our Day," p. 125.) Bruno Bettelheim has documented the regressive, infantile behavior of Nazi concentration camp inmates whose dependence on their guards and the camp administrators led to grotesque and tragic imitation and admiration of them, based on the tacit assumption that "since they are so powerful, they must be right." A Chinese respondent relates the "great sense of relief" upon the completion of thought reform: "They had passed through their trial [Lifton paraphrases his remarks] and made their symbolic submission; and many—especially among the young—seemed to feel that a closer bond had been established between themselves and the government." (Lifton, *Thought Reform*, p. 270.) The fascination of intellectuals with Communism sometimes exhibits some of the same features.

least likely to yield this result, for it typically destabilizes expectations, whose certainty the "authoritarian personality" presumably craves even more than others do;

(4) the Chinese strategy of "thought reform," whose end product in theory is a complete acceptance of official beliefs and attitudes.

Finally, one should add another situation in which

(5) diffuse support is proffered in spite of terror; the experience of many former inmates of prisons and concentration camps suggests the frequency with which even the victims themselves continue to be fundamentally loyal to the system, with legitimating forces overriding the impact of terror.[8]

It is important, however, to bear in mind the frequency and impact of the reverse effect, too. Surface conformity makes for a tacit code of mimicking obedience that typically generates a universe of cant. As a Hungarian intellectual later reminisced,

Eighty per cent of what an average person speaks in a day is a sheer lie. . . . It was this abnormal situation . . . the necessity of telling lies hour after hour, day in and day out, the need to keep constant track of one's own lies, so as to avoid being caught in gross contradictions, that caused us intense physical pain and exhaustion.[9]

This is after all what Boris Pasternak's Zhivago tells Dudorov and Gordon shortly before his death: "The great majority of us are required to live a life of constant, systematic duplicity. Your health is bound to be affected if, day after day, you say the opposite of what you feel, if you grovel before what you dislike and rejoice at what brings you nothing but misfortune."[10] Anatolii Kuznetsov, the Soviet writer, exclaimed after leaving his homeland in 1969:

Life is like some constant unbroken theatrical production. You never say out loud what you really think, only what you ought to say. . . . Insofar as we have to live in that theater, every person has a sort of

---

[8] See, for example, Beck and Godin, *Russian Purge*. This was generally true of the Soviet military commanders imprisoned in 1936–41 but released and restored to active service after the German invasion. It also applies to Trotsky's attitude toward the Soviet system despite his own exile and persecution.
[9] Interview protocol, Columbia University Research Project on Hungary (1957), unpublished.
[10] *Doctor Zhivago*, p. 483.

collection of phrases which he speaks and says publicly, and a corresponding collection of actions. For a normal human being, it is extremely difficult to lead such a double life.[11]

And Stalin's daughter notes that "the ugliest feature of Soviet life was the endless dissimulation and double-facedness infused into the Soviet people from their schoolroom days, so that it became almost second nature."[12]

Moreover, when terror is used on a mass scale by a regime perceived to be illegitimate, as was the case in Hungary before 1956, once the pressure is removed, instead of substantial support what is revealed is profound rot. Indeed, the very mimicry contributes to the process, as it did there, producing a collapse of institutions and official values once the population perceives that it can with impunity shed the protective camouflage of its "outer" personality. That, of course, was not the case in the Soviet Union, where stability was maintained.

The Costs of Terror

The price of terror is legion, its victims forever unknown. The cost in human lives is the most obvious, but estimates of casualties vary too much to permit meaningful interpretation. The number of those arrested, exiled to labor camps, and subjected to penalties and persecution is not even approximately known. And beyond all these is the vast mass of citizens at large who were, or are, in some unrecorded way, subjected to the diffuse impact of terror.

The most visible objects of terror are members of "alien" classes, of proscribed groups, sometimes ethnic, sometimes religious, and former members of other political parties. Ignoring variations from country to country, one might find that in gross numbers, after the initial consolidation of revolutionary power, the peasantry has suffered in the course of collectivization but has otherwise been relatively immune to political terror. All in

[11] Columbia Broadcasting Company, "The Ordeal of Anatoly Kuznetsov," CBS-TV, Sept. 2, 1969.
[12] Alliluyeva, *Only One Year*, pp. 178–79.

all, industrial labor has probably suffered somewhat less. First, unlike the dispersed peasantry, no organizational breakthrough was needed to gain control over factory workers. Second, a vague ideological commitment to the proletariat contributed to the decisions of Soviet and East European leaders to force the peasantry to bear the brunt of developmental sacrifices. On the other hand, during the takeover stage, in Soviet Russia for instance, there were quite a few victims among the workers— active trade-unionists, cadres of anarchists, Mensheviks, Social-ist-Revolutionaries, and other groups. Clearly the exigencies of power overrode ideological commitments. Officials and cadres of all sorts, from notables to lower level party, police, army, and managerial personnel, have provided a relatively high number of victims, as has the intelligentsia. It is in the nature of terror, however, that it also strikes without obvious reason in categor-ical or judicial terms.

There is not enough "hard" information to differentiate with regard to the effectiveness of terror, but it appears that it has been most telling (in Hungary, at least) among the bureaucracy —those who most directly depend on the regime for success and status. Terror is perhaps least effective against those who have the least to lose—some of the inmates of prisons and camps, and to some extent intellectuals and students. It evidently succeeds in cutting word-of-mouth communication among workers more fully than among intellectuals, though there are examples of surreptitious contact among laborers in the same enterprise (in the Soviet Union and in Czechoslovakia) at the height of the purges.

Though terror may effectively perform its functions, it is wasteful and inefficient. The total strain on and disruption of production, services, research, and communications are among its more obvious concomitants. But terror is not easily adminis-tered with discretion. While making extensive use of terror, So-viet public administration has generally sought a formula that would "guarantee both the loyalty and the efficiency" of the apparatus[13]—something it could never find. Only at a later point, typically after the mobilization stage, does the priority in official values shift so as to give greater weight to efficiency.[14] As John Dewey observed, "efficiency requires methods which will enlist greater individual interest and attention, greater emotional and intellectual liberty," something that is almost impossible to produce with the extensive use of terror.[15]

Similarly, terror renders rational administration and precision in planning impossible; hence the call for regularity and predictability that typically precedes or accompanies its abandonment. Then there is the possible growth of the machinery of coercion as a privileged and expanding empire. Its scope is well dramatized in this vignette by the correspondent of the Communist London *Daily Worker* who went to witness the Hungarian crisis of 1956:

> There were Gestapo-like torture chambers with whips and gallows and instruments for crushing people's limbs. There were tiny punishment cells. There were piles of letters from abroad, intercepted for censorship. There were batteries of tape-recorders to take down telephone conversations. There were prostitutes retained as police spies and agents-provocateurs. And the young brutes who made up this strong arm of the people's democratic state were paid—according to documents found on their dead bodies—3,000 to 4,000 forints a month as men, 9,000 to 12,000 as officers; 3 to 12 times the average wage. Plus luxurious flats while thousands in Budapest lived cramped in slums and cellars.[16]

The impact of terror on the political process includes, of course, the constriction of candid information; the widespread falsification of official, even internal, reports; the myth of official infallibility that makes questioning of policies dangerous; the recruitment of opportunists into the elite and bureaucracy. But in all these regards it is hard to draw the line between the effects of structural features of the system as such, and of terror in particular.

[13] See Fainsod, *How Russia Is Ruled*, rev. ed., p. 398.
[14] See, for example, George Feiwel, *The Soviet Quest for Economic Efficiency.*
[15] Dewey, "Force and Coercion," p. 366.
[16] Peter Fryer, *Hungarian Tragedy*, pp. 36–37.

The harmful impact of terror in the international standing of Communist polities also requires no elaboration. Both Russia in the 1930's and China in the 1960's suffered in prestige and influence as a consequence of their domestic purges. And, as Soviet critics did not tire to point out after 1955, the purges in the high command seriously jeopardized Soviet defensive capabilities once the German attack came in 1941.

As for the effect of terror on the individual, one general consequence, with high social costs, is the prevalence of deception. As a high Soviet party official put it, recalling the effects of the Great Suspicion that had blanketed the land, the regime had mistrusted the peasantry with the result that "kolkhoz managers and farmers, too, lost their sense of being masters of the land. . . . It undermined their sense of truth and honesty."[17] Similarly, the typical "deprivation of individual autonomy" and the trend toward brutalization, servility, and corruption are among the common but costly concomitants of terror.[18] All this says nothing of the erratic, hysterical, or paralyzing effects of terror once it exceeds the bounds of functionality. Refugees from Communist countries have almost invariably cited terror and the secret police as their primary grievance against the system. Whatever allowance one may wish to make for the selectivity of the sample and *post facto* exaggeration, there remains a consistency of response—regardless of state of origin, nationality, class, age, or occupation—too overwhelming to be dismissed. This is true, for example, of the large group of refugees from the Soviet Union interviewed in 1950–52,[19] as well as of the Hungarian refugees after 1956.[20]

[17] G. S. Zolotukhin (First Secretary of Tambov *Obkom* and member of Central Committee, CPSU), "Stavka na doverie."
[18] Brzezinski, *The Soviet Bloc*, p. 141; Zinner, *Revolution in Hungary*, pp. 114ff.
[19] Inkeles and Bauer, *The Soviet Citizen*, pp. 246–47, 270. Among a large sample, "security from arbitrary interference and punishment" was offered very frequently as essential for an ideal political system. An arrest history, either of the respondent or of members of his family, was found to have been more productive of alienation than other obvious causes such as a low standard of living. And of those who by their own statements had once been in favor of the Soviet regime but had turned against it, terror was uniformly and by far the single most frequent reason volunteered by the respondents.
[20] As one analyst put it, "the two aspects that are constantly arising are the universality of the machinery of political control and the arbitrary way in which victims

Communists themselves assessed terror similarly in the subsequent years of de-Stalinization. Nikita Khrushchev's "secret" speech to the Twentieth Party Congress in 1956 epitomizes this reaction to the years of terror:

Mass arrests of Party, Soviet, economic and military workers caused tremendous harm to our country and to the cause of socialist advancement. Mass repressions had a negative influence on the moral-political condition of the Party, created a situation of uncertainty, contributed to the spreading of unhealthy suspicion, and sowed distrust among communists. All sorts of slanderers and careerists were active.... There is no doubt that our march forward toward socialism and toward the preparation for the country's defense would have been much more successful were it not for the tremendous loss in the cadres suffered as a result of baseless and false mass repressions in 1937–38....

Very grievous consequences, especially in reference to the beginning of the war, followed Stalin's annihilation of many military commanders and political workers during 1937–1941 because of his suspiciousness and through slanderous accusations.... The policy of large-scale repression against the military cadres led also to undermined military discipline, because for several years officers of all ranks and even soldiers in the Party and Komsomol cells were taught to "unmask" their superiors as hidden enemies.[21]

Another indictment circulated but no longer permitted to be published in Moscow came more recently from one of the Soviet Union's outstanding scientists, Andrei Sakharov, who was moved to write that Stalin's "hypocrisy and demagogy"

served as a convenient screen for ... the treacherous and sudden use of the machinery of torture, execution, and informants, intimidating and making fools of millions of people, the majority of whom were neither cowards nor fools. As a consequence of this "specific feature"

---

of penalization appear to have been chosen." When each respondent was asked to check the most important and least important among fifteen listed areas of deprivation or grievances in pre–1956 Hungary, "in terms of total mentions, 'fear of arrest and terror' was an easy winner." (John Madge, "Attitudes of Refugee Respondents," pp. 48, 57–58.) Another study of Hungarian refugees, conducted independently, found "a long-term and insurmountable feeling of personal insecurity" and a "profound sense of frustration" among key motives for revolutionary behavior in 1956. (Lawrence Hinkle, "Health, Human Ecology, and the Hungarian Revolution," pp. 4, 7.)

It is probably significant, however, that terror ranked relatively low among the many complaints voiced during the short-lived Hundred Flowers campaign in China in 1957, when overt criticism, even by non-Communists, was temporarily tolerated and even encouraged. An extensive collection of critical statements does include a few relevant comments, as reported in the Chinese press, mostly made by alienated academics. (Roderick MacFarquhar, *The Hundred Flowers Campaign and the Chinese Intellectuals,* pp. 87–114, 145, 196.)

[21] *The Anti-Stalin Campaign and International Communism,* pp. 38–39, 48–49.

of Stalinism, it was the Soviet people, its most active, talented, and honest representatives, who suffered the most terrible blow.

At least ten to fifteen million people perished in the torture chambers of the NKVD from torture and execution, in camps for exiled kulaks and so-called semi-kulaks and members of their families. . . . People perished in the mines of Norilsk and Vorkuta from freezing, starvation, and exhausting labor, at countless construction projects, in timber-cutting, building of canals, or simply during transportation in prison trains, in the overcrowded holds of "death ships" in the Sea of Okhotsk, and during the settlement of entire peoples.

After similarly reciting the killing of military commanders, the damage done to agriculture by Stalinist terror, and other "monstrosities" of the recent past, Sakharov admonishes his fellow citizens not to relent in the exposure and analysis of Stalinism:

We are often told lately not to "rub salt into wounds." This is usually being said by people who suffered no wounds. Actually only the most meticulous analysis of the past and its consequences will now enable us to wash off the blood and dirt that befouled our banner. . . . We are learning to express our opinions, without taking the lead from the bosses and without fearing for our lives.[22]

Such assessments could be multiplied many times over. They recur in memoirs, works of fiction, letters to the editor, and partially clandestine proclamations of Soviet and East European intellectuals.[23] One of the most eloquent of such recent docu-

[22] *Progress, Coexistence and Intellectual Freedom*, pp. 52–56.

[23] A sample of Soviet anti-Stalinist historiography, Alexander Nekrich's *June 22, 1941*, which became the object of bitter political controversy, provides the following judgment: "The economy of the Soviet state could have developed faster still and achieved an even higher level by the time the war started, if the situation in the country had not been adversely affected by the cult of personality and, in connection with it, by the groundless mass repressions conducted by J. V. Stalin against Party and Soviet officials . . . [which] made the country feverish, interfered with the development of production, introduced fear and uncertainty, fettered initiative. Managers of enterprises were replaced one after another. The new people coming into managerial positions in the economy often did not possess the necessary experience and knowledge. The atmosphere of spy-mania, artificially created by J. V. Stalin, strengthened suspicion and opened doors for ambitious men and lickspittles, for unprincipled people and careerists, for self-seekers and slanderers. Under these conditions one needed a certain measure of courage to take responsibility for some industrial innovation or other, particularly if its advantages would not become apparent right away. Many enterprise managers avoided innovations for this reason, preferring to live quietly so as not to risk being accused of wrecking." (Vladimir Petrov, ed., *June 22, 1941*, pp. 112–13.) See also a transcript of the stormy discussion of Nekrich's book at the Moscow Institute of Marxism-Leninism, in *ibid.*, pp. 257–58. For other comments, see, for example, Imre Nagy, *On Communism*; Kaplan, "Zamyšlení nad politickými procesy"; and the writings of as varied a group as Palmiro Togliatti, Adam Schaff, Milovan Djilas, and György Lukács.

ments, after detailing seventeen "charges" against Stalin, warns in conclusion against a return to "the sinister atmosphere of suspicion and fear of the police, the consequences of which have apparently not yet been overcome."[24]

The Balance Sheet

The foregoing sketch of some of the consequences of the use of political terror leaves unanswered the question of the relation of benefits to costs. Perhaps the logical approach, given the "functional" orientation of this study, would be to weigh functional against dysfunctional outcomes. But how to tell one from the other? It is not just that the standard definition of functionality in terms of adaptation seems peculiarly unsuited here, for adaptation to terror would make complete surrender to the system the most functional of all courses for the citizen to pursue. There is both a general problem of assigning "functionality" and a specific one of applying the notion to political terror. There is always, Robert Merton has suggested, "the difficult problem of developing an organon for assessing the net balance of consequences." Moreover, "in any given instance, an item may have both functional and dysfunctional consequences, giving rise to the difficult and important problem of evolving canons for assessing the net balance of the aggregations of consequences." Finally, "items may be functional for some individuals and subgroups and dysfunctional for others."[25] We are thus left in search of criteria for sorting the consequences. Here a major difficulty stems from the fact that whether or not a given effect is considered a plus or a minus ultimately depends on the values that the observer attaches to the variables and goals. To Communist policy-makers themselves what was judged desirable at one stage may have seemed counterproductive later, when the full consequences could be seen. Even to an outsider the balance of considerations may appear very different de-

[24] Piotr Yakir, letter to the editor of *Kommunist* (Moscow).
[25] Merton, *On Theoretical Sociology*, pp. 90, 105, 106.

pending on his time-perspective: what seems functional within a limited time perspective may prove dysfunctional over the long haul, and vice versa.[26]

Because we find ourselves unable responsibly to pursue this line of analysis, we may turn to another, more limited approach. One possible criterion is the total effect, once terror disappears, on what might be called the commitment-alienation quotient. Here one can readily think of two diametrically opposed possibilities: successful accommodation and socialization, ritualization of belief, and adequate functional equivalents, making for stronger normative attachment to the regime; or a political outburst, a breakdown of institutions and official values, a sudden realization that "the emperor has never worn any clothes." Characteristically, we have seen examples of both outcomes. If Hungary in 1956 exemplified the second, as we saw, the Soviet Union with some reservations typified the first. Once again, terror proves to be ambiguous in its effects.

If, then, we ask whether terror is necessary or essential for a Communist regime, we can point back to our earlier conclusion that totalitarianism does indeed imply arbitrary and severe coercion. In other words, at the mobilization stage of its development a Communist polity committed to the exercise of total control and the prompt implementation of sweeping change does require purposive terror. A commitment to these two goals is neither necessary nor inevitable, but once it is made, terror follows with iron logic. Even then, not all terror wielded

---

[26] Nor is the problem eased by what we have earlier posited as the ambiguity of terror—its alienation- and support-generating effects; and the obvious impossibility of "replaying" the sequence of events leaving out terror. We might specify arbitrarily that functionality is to be judged by the balance of supportive as against alienating consequences. Or we might label dysfunctional those situations in which the total hostile affect generated by the application of terror exceeds the support generated (or their inverse removed) thereby. Or we could take as the test the question of how to increase the system's capacity to act without generating countercurrents of equal or greater magnitude (as suggested by Etzioni, *The Active Society*, p. 352). But in all these instances the operational impossibility of a quantitative assessment remains: we would need a measure of cumulative compliance, divided by cumulative alienation; and even if we could find it, we could not isolate the specific weight of terror from that of other simultaneous processes. For assessments of the utility and limits of functional analysis, see N. J. Demerath and R. A. Peterson, eds., *System, Change, and Conflict*; C. G. Hempel, "The Logic of Functional Analysis"; and A. J. Gregor, "Political Science and the Uses of Functional Analysis."

by a Communist regime can be adjudged to have been "essential." Recalling the three operations most costly in human lives, we must reaffirm our earlier assessment. Forced collectivization, as and when envisaged by Stalin, was *not* essential, for the same goals could probably have been attained at lesser cost, with less violence, less disruption, and less traumatic effects. But once forced collectivization was begun, it was impossible to conduct without terror, though even then greater skill, sensitivity, and patience might have significantly reduced the number of victims. To be sure, "it is difficult to convince people of the need for new habits and discipline exclusively by methods of persuasion."[27] Even an evolutionary change in the rural social structure and in urban-rural terms of trade would have required some coercive compliance. Yet it is undeniable that the escalation of coercion into both situational terror and purposive liquidation of the kulaks was not essential to the realization of Soviet economic goals.

Similarly, the Great Purge in the Soviet Union cannot be justified by the priority goal of economic development: it came after the critical breakthrough. Nor can it be justified by the existence of a real threat to the system or the leadership that the terror sought to remove: the Great Purge came after the most serious and potentially dangerous opposition within the Soviet elite had been defeated by Stalin, and struck at many who by any objective criterion were guiltless. Thus Hannah Arendt is led to conclude that "none of these immense sacrifices in human life was motivated by a *raison d'état*."[28]

Finally, in the case of the rural violence in China in 1950–51,

[27] C. K. Wilber, *The Soviet Model and Underdeveloped Countries*, p. 129. Wilber (p. 222) argues against the rejection of the Soviet model of development *in toto* where it is rooted in failure "to differentiate between the essential and accidental aspects of Soviet experience."

[28] *Totalitarianism*, pp. xv–xvi, 19. Similarly, Aron (*Démocratie et totalitarisme*, pp. 275–302) argues that, whereas terror at the takeover stage was "normal" and terror against the kulaks was at least "rational," the purges of 1936–38 were unreasonable or irrational: they were not required for the regime's security, nor for the advance toward preconceived, revolutionary transformation goals. The fact that the purges were not intended to facilitate socioeconomic development is also illustrated by the liquidation of numerous foreign Communists and Comintern officials. See Branko Lazitch, "Le martyrologie du Comintern."

the attacks on the landlords were not undertaken out of a sense of essential social engineering, nor as a security measure. As we have pointed out before, Maoism professed to know ways and means of reeducating members of even hostile classes rather than liquidating them; the terror campaign was essentially a policy, for which there were viable alternatives, calculated to maximize peasant support for the Communist regime and turn the rural population against the landlords. Land reform served the two general functions of establishing Communist political control in the countryside, for which terror seems to have been a necessity, though not in all its excesses, and encouraging economic development, which hardly required the use of terror.[29]

Variables and Variations

Significant differences among the various extant Communist regimes have been noted throughout this book. We have assumed that in each instance the deviation from what we have considered an ideal type has been due to intervening variables susceptible to identification and analysis. At the same time, the limited nature of the "sample" of Communist polities, the simultaneous influence of numerous variables, and other methodological problems such as weighting of different factors, force the following discussion to be somewhat impressionistic and tentative: we must beware of spurious precision and finality. Though some of the variables tend to occur in interrelated and interacting clusters, it is simplest to present them one by one.

Historical sequence. That the Soviet Union was the first among Communist states to follow an uncharted path not only imposed special hardships on it but, more important, permitted the regimes that came later to learn from some of the Soviet errors (notably in regard to collectivization) and to avoid them.

Mode of takeover. Whether the regime came to power by a coup, by protracted civil war, or by bureaucratic means (in

[29] See the illuminating article by Ezra Vogel, "Land Reform in Kwangtung, 1951–1953"; and Charles Hoffman, *Work Incentive Practices and Policies.*

"derivative" regimes under Soviet auspices) appears to have had only indirect influence on the level of terror. For example, the role of the civil war experience in shaping the values of the political elite, as in China and Yugoslavia, and the particular experience of the "derivative" regimes, which, tied to the Soviet Union, experienced only an abortive mobilization stage, resulted in a compressed period for transformations, with less time for socialization and accommodation to take effect. The additional element of anti-Soviet sentiment provided first a further source of alienation and later another impetus for normative identification and integration on a national basis.

Level of socioeconomic development. On the one hand, relative underdevelopment prior to the mobilization stage does not seem to have been a handicap in establishing totalitarian control; if anything, China produced a higher level of organizational penetration than Russia. This would seem to contradict the notion that modern technology and economy are prerequisites for effective totalitarianism; on the contrary, industrialization and modernization emerge as consequences rather than as preconditions for Communist totalitarianism. On the other hand, we do not find a clear correlation between levels of development and of terror. At one end of the spectrum, societies closest to the subsistence level have built-in limits to the amount of disruption they can tolerate, limits set for them by their economic level. At the other, the two most highly developed states, Czechoslovakia and East Germany, both experienced relatively less terror at the mobilization stage than did most other Communist systems. Indirectly, of course, underlying differences between the Soviet and Chinese patterns and world views have been importantly influenced by differential levels of development,[30] with consequences for the use of terror as well.

Political stability and social cohesion. A high level of political stability seems to relate to another important variable, organizational development, but stability is not itself an obvious de-

---

[30] See, for example, Richard Lowenthal, "Soviet and Chinese World Views."

terminant of the level of terror. However, political instability does appear to be responsible for inducing a low level of terror: except for the special and first case of the Soviet Union, all the relevant countries (Poland, East Germany, perhaps North Korea and Cuba) were among those that used the least terror at the mobilization stage. Inversely, of the Communist states with stable conditions (with the possible exception of Mongolia and, because of its different strategy, China) not one was among those experiencing a low level of terror. The relative degree of social cohesion prior to forced transformation from above, however, does not appear to have had any clear influence on the pattern of terror.

Speed and sequence or synchronization of directed change. The evidence suggests strongly that greater speed as well as greater synchronization of transformation processes imposed from above requires disproportionately more extensive and/or intensive terror.

Organization level. Differences in organizational penetration, discipline, and density (between the Soviet Union and China, for example) are of prime importance, especially in rural transformation, in determining the level of terror required. The differences in Eastern Europe in this regard are also significant, but they are at times obscured by the role of the Red Army or the threat of Soviet "presence," which acted as a functional equivalent of administrative penetration. Perhaps the clearest case of this variable at work is Poland, where the low level of organizational penetration and the low level of support were causally related to the elite's resistance to public purge trials and to collectivization.

External "threat." The perception of external threats, not normally a critical variable, is likely to add to the pressure for speedier mobilization and change, as in Russia in the 1930's. It is more important in times of crisis when it provides an element of community between elite and mass, making for greater regime legitimacy and hence the readier availability of normative equivalents to terror. The double experience of Yugoslavia—against Germany and Italy in World War II, and against the Soviet Union during the "cold war" from 1948 on—seems revealing in this regard.

Traditional political culture. Although the relevance of traditional values has been stressed in the text (in particular, in explaining the special orientation of the Chinese Communist leadership), it remains true that the impact of this variable has been selective and that rather similar strands of tradition could be identified with other cultures.[31] Moreover, traditional political culture appears to have had little weight unless it has also influenced the new ruling elite. Thus, the heritage of political violence in Bulgaria and Yugoslavia has not made for higher levels of terror there than in other Communist polities.

National experience and elite values. The particular experiences of Communist elites, as in Russia and China, for example, are quite important in accounting for variations among Communist states. The nationalist "normative equivalent" earlier mentioned becomes operational only once it is shared by the political elite, as in Rumania, for example. Moreover, the abandonment of both coercive mobilization and terror by the Yugoslav leadership after the break with the Soviet Union was due to a combination of "objective," situational factors and the particular "subjective" outlook and experience of the Yugoslav elite. Finally, the resistance of the Polish Communist leadership to large-scale terror after its consolidation in power was presumably traceable first to the lingering effects of the liquidation of the Polish Communist leadership by Stalin in 1938, and second to the persistence of such autonomous authorities and organizations within Poland as the Catholic Church, which the party leadership was reluctant to attack directly.

The dictator. When all is said and done, the individual leader of a given Communist polity may provide personal qualities that can override all other patterns and regularities. Indeed, this seeming ability to defy secular trends contributes to his illusion of his own omnipotence.

---

[31] Platonism, for example. See Friedrich, "Totalitarianism: Recent Trends," p. 35.

Support, compliance, and alienation. Although occasionally we have referred to what we believe have been marked variations in the degree of legitimacy enjoyed and compliance received by Communist regimes, we must confess to our inability to produce a precise indicator of commitment or alienation.

Exogenous elements. Variations among Communist polities are of course further affected by the occasional intervention of outside forces to arrest or inhibit what would have developed into new and different variants. Soviet intervention in Hungary in 1956 and in Czechoslovakia in 1968 are the prime examples of forcibly arrested development. It might be added that, ironically, there is no comparable case of direct intervention by non-Communist powers nor any instance of political suicide by Communist regimes (except for isolated experiments especially at the subnational level).

Prospects and Lessons

The trend away from political terror at the post-mobilization stage is unmistakable, but it is not a consistent, simple, or linear process, and the record is still too fresh and sketchy to reveal the full range of alternative ways it may evolve. Whether and in what form the use of terror may be revived will depend on the structural features of the political and economic systems, and the will of the policy-making elites. As social scientists we cannot predict that a given leader will choose to ignore the enormous costs of a return to mass terror. Yet, assuming a measure of rationality on the part of future decision-makers, and assuming that their priorities coincide roughly with those we have imputed to them, the fate of terror is likely to follow in large measure the fate of the polity as a whole.[32] As Merle Fainsod has suggested with regard to another crucial area of unintended change in Communist systems: "Whether the transformation of a mobilizing party into an adaptive party will operate as a threat to the system's dynamism is not easily determinable. It may well

---

[32] Friedrich (*ibid.*, pp. 37–38) is even prepared to suggest that a Communist system might afford to permit freedom of expression so long as its taboos are respected and there is no organization of dissent.

be that the successful management and direction of a complex and sophisticated industrial society offers no other alternative."[33] Similarly, it is likely that there is no rational alternative to the abandonment of terror: how ironic that a system that has pursued a strategy of confronting its citizenry with "the dilemma of one alternative" must find itself faced with a similar dilemma!

Although a return to mass terror is not an absolute impossibility, even under an "adaptive" regime, such a reversal is highly improbable in Communist states that have moved beyond the mobilization stage. It appears to us that this is due above all to the combination of a political elite in which elements of pluralism, oligarchy, collectivity in decision-making, or some form of interest-group representation will tend to persist and grow, and an awareness within the society at large and the elite in particular of the inordinately high social, economic, and political costs of terror, which in an increasingly modernized society are bound to clash with the values of a significant part of both mass and elite.

No stable formula of governance, no modal mix of sanctions and incentives is yet detectable for these polities. As before, Communist policy-makers will typically continue to face difficult choices. The pressures to avoid coercive power can be expected to multiply further, but the growth of dissent and deviance under conditions of continued scarcity of alternative forms of power is likely to impress some leaders with the high cost of not resorting to terror, too. However, intuitively as well as rationally, both among the survivors of the Stalin era and in the younger generations, individuals and groups in the elite are bound to conclude that the costs of terror far exceed its gains. Hence, to revive mass terror as a means of policy would first require the removal of such people and the reemergence of a single dictator answerable to no one. The thrust of our argument has been to show that, despite zigzags and contradictions, the dynamics of the system point in the opposite direction. We hasten to add that, although modernization may prohibitively

[33] "Transformations in the CPSU," pp. 68–69.

raise the costs and an awareness of the costs of a return to mass terror, social and economic development by no means assures the adoption of the rule of law, let alone a transition to political democracy.[34]

Yet what could be more foolish than to smugly write off terror as a passing or already past phase of Communist development in distant lands? In its willful tragedy and horror Communist terror has few parallels in history, but it is also true that terror has been a hallmark of all societies, from the primitive to the industrial. The celebration of intolerance in the name of fanatical attachment to a cause has marked a sadly recurrent pattern throughout the ages of mankind. The fates of Socrates, Jesus, and Galileo, the Inquisition, and the French Revolution are but some of its better-known milestones. They bear witness that "there is no more lamentable lesson to be culled from history than that contained in her inability to furnish a single instance of a religion accepted with unquestioning sincerity and fervor which did not, out of these very qualities, beget intolerance."[35] Whereas mere intolerance is of course a far cry from the Great Terror that befell Russia in the 1930's or the Cultural Revolution that struck China in the 1960's, the injection of a quasi-religious fanaticism into politics when combined with the use of terror tends to produce a reign of terror.

In a setting of rapid directed change toward ideologically prescribed goals, the energizing effects of commitment and zeal, the self-righteousness of the "ins" toward the "outs," the paranoid propensities of such dogmas, the sense of urgency that justifies all means, the pretense of logic and inevitability, can combine to make many a "captive mind" rationalize as sensible and necessary the most absurd and outrageous deeds. Once initiated, terror tends to become habit-forming and self-perpetuating; traditional norms and defenses against violence break down; resistance to terror lends justification to its perpetuation; guilt by association and institutionalized suspicion

---

[34] See also Reinhard Bendix, *Nation-Building and Citizenship*, pp. 62ff.
[35] Rafael Sabatini, *Torquemada and the Spanish Inquisition*, p. 3.

spread a pall of anxiety; and soon terrified men come to engage in needless cruelty.[36]

Forced change, in an atmosphere of ideological dedication, is then apt to release the basest instincts of the implementors. To the victims, who invariably include men of goodwill, the process must seem incredible and absurd. Koestler's Rubashov, upon hearing the monstrous charges made against him, was struck by "this mixture of logic and absurdity."[37] Indeed, the tragedy is epitomized by the Kafkaesque tension between the element of the absurd and the element of the rational. Who indeed can fail to despair over "that secret complicity that joins the logical and the everyday to the tragic"?[38]

We are then led to conclude with Charles Wilber that "if the social costs of the Stalin era had to be repeated when utilizing the Soviet model [elsewhere], then almost any alternative would be preferable." But it is well to remember, too, that "there is insufficient evidence to say that the *process* of development *required* these human costs."[39] One lesson of the Communist experience is that brutal excesses are not necessarily inherent in the concept of politically induced change.[40]

In an age of violence and anxiety, there are in the experience of Communist systems other lessons worth pondering, too. Not the least of these are the alienating and self-defeating consequences of coercion pushed beyond definite limits. But their experience also shows that people can be led to change their behavior patterns, provided the change is not overly rapid, is accompanied by adequate material and normative rewards, and does not challenge the central values of their existence.[41]

---

[36] Engles wrote Marx on Sept. 4, 1870: "*La terreur*—that is mostly needless cruelty practised by terrified men." (Marx and Engels, *Werke*, XXXIII, 53.)

[37] *Darkness at Noon*, p. 135. Aron (*Démocratie et totalitarisme*, pp. 286–87) is similarly moved to say that under Stalin "one lived in a strange world which gave a meaning to every event but whose totality was absurd."

[38] Albert Camus, "Hope and the Absurd in the Work of Franz Kafka," in his *The Myth of Sisyphus*, p. 128.

[39] Wilber, *The Soviet Model*, pp. 125–26.

[40] See J. W. Lewis, "Social Limits of Politically Induced Change."

[41] On the basis of the Soviet and Chinese experiences one may well assert, for instance, that it is just not true that peasants can never be made to pool their efforts without duress and that therefore cooperativization must imply terror.

If modernizing and modernized societies require an unprece-
dented concentration of power, the Communist experience underscores once again the all-important necessity of subjecting
that power to continual accountability. But it also reinforces
our conviction that the struggle for the minds of men must be
fought and won well short of any effort at "total control." Such
an effort, whatever its goals, is in any case bound to be self-defeating: forces inherent in the process of modernization tend
ultimately to frustrate totalitarian aspirations.

When György Fáludi, the Hungarian poet, was sentenced
to be executed without cause, he scribbled in his own blood,
"Orwell was right." Today we can see better, perhaps, that
fortunately Orwell was wrong. Like the Abbé Sieyès, the societies that have witnessed the terror have survived to share the
future of mankind.

Bibliography

Bibliography

Alliluyeva, Svetlana. *Only One Year*. New York: Harper and Row, 1969.

Almond, Gabriel A., ed. *The Struggle for Democracy in Germany*. Chapel Hill: University of North Carolina Press, 1949.

Almond, Gabriel A., and G. Bingham Powell. *Comparative Politics*. Boston: Little, Brown, 1966.

The Anti-Stalin Campaign and International Communism. (Pub. by Russian Inst.) New York: Columbia University Press, 1956.

Apter, David E. *The Politics of Modernization*. Chicago: University of Chicago Press, 1965.

Arendt, Hannah. *The Origins of Totalitarianism*, rev. ed. New York: Harcourt, Brace, 1968.

——. "Reflections on Violence," *Journal of International Affairs*, XXIII, 1 (1969).

Aron, Raymond. *Démocratie et totalitarisme*. Paris: Gallimard, 1965.

Aronson, Gregor, et al., eds. *Russian Jewry 1917–1967*. New York: Thomas Yoseloff, 1969.

Azrael, Jeremy. "Is Coercion Withering Away?" *Problems of Communism*, XI, 6 (Nov.–Dec. 1962).

Baker, George W., and Dwight W. Chapman, eds., *Man and Society in Disaster*. New York: Basic Books, 1962.

Barghoorn, Frederick C. "The Security Police," in Skilling and Griffiths, listed below.

Barnett, A. Doak. *Cadres, Bureaucracy, and Political Power in Communist China*. New York: Columbia University Press, 1967.

——. *China on the Eve of Communist Takeover*. New York: Praeger, 1963.

——, ed. *Chinese Communist Politics in Action*. Seattle: University of Washington Press, 1969.

——. *Communist China: The Early Years*. New York: Praeger, 1966.

Beck, Carl. "Bureaucracy and Political Development in Eastern Europe," in LaPalombara, listed below.

Beck, F., and W. Godin (pseuds.). *Russian Purge and the Extraction of Confession.* New York: Viking, 1951.

Bendix, Reinhard. *Nation-Building and Citizenship.* New York: Wiley, 1964.

Berkowitz, Leonard, ed. *Advances in Experimental Social Psychology,* vol. III. New York: Academic Press, 1967.

Berman, Harold J. *Justice in the USSR,* rev. ed. New York: Vintage, 1963.

Berman, Harold J., and James W. Spindler. "Soviet Comrades' Courts," *Washington Law Review,* XXXVIII, 4 (Winter 1963).

Bernstein, Thomas P. "Leadership and Mass Mobilization in the Soviet and Chinese Collectivization Campaigns of 1929–30 and 1955–56: A Comparison," *China Quarterly,* 31 (July–Sept. 1967).

Bialer, Seweryn, ed. *Stalin and His Generals.* New York: Pegasus, 1969.

Bienen, Henry. *Violence and Social Change.* Chicago: University of Chicago Press, 1968.

Black, Cyril E., and Thomas P. Thornton, eds. *Communism and Revolution.* Princeton: Princeton University Press, 1964.

Brabec, V. "The Relationship of the CPCS and the Public to the Political Trials of the Early Fifties," *Revue Dejin Socialismu* (Prague), 3 (July 1969); Engl. trans. in Radio Free Europe, *Czechoslovak Press Survey,* no. 2275 (Nov. 25, 1969).

Bramsted, Ernest K. *Goebbels and National Socialist Propaganda 1925–1945.* East Lansing: Michigan State University Press, 1965.

Brandt, Conrad, John K. Fairbank, and Benjamin Schwartz, eds. *A Documentary History of Chinese Communism.* Cambridge, Mass.: Harvard University Press, 1952.

Brehm, Jack W., and Arthur R. Cohen. *Explorations in Cognitive Dissonance.* New York: Wiley, 1962.

Bridgham, Philip. "Mao's 'Cultural Revolution': Origin and Development," *China Quarterly,* 29 (Jan.–Mar. 1967).

Brown, James F. *The New Eastern Europe.* New York: Praeger, 1966.

Brzezinski, Zbigniew. *The Permanent Purge.* Cambridge, Mass.: Harvard University Press, 1956.

———. *The Soviet Bloc,* rev. ed. Cambridge, Mass.: Harvard University Press, 1968.

———. "The Soviet Political System: Transformation or Degeneration," *Problems of Communism,* XV, 1 (Jan. 1966).

Burks, R. V. "Eastern Europe," in Black and Thornton, listed above.

Bychowski, Gustav. *Dictators and Disciples.* New York: International Universities Press, 1948.

Calvert, Noris Peter. "Revolution: The Politics of Violence," *Political Studies*, XV, 1 (Feb. 1967).

Camus, Albert. *The Myth of Sisyphus.* New York: Knopf, 1955.

Carr, E. H. *A History of Soviet Russia.* London: Macmillan, vol. I 1950, vol. II 1952.

Chamberlin, William Henry. *The Russian Revolution.* 2 vols. New York: Macmillan, 1935.

Chang, Parris H. "Mao's Great Purge: A Political Balance Sheet," *Problems of Communism*, XVIII, 2 (Mar.–Apr. 1969).

Chapman, Dwight W. "Dimensions of Models in Disaster Behavior," in Baker and Chapman, listed above.

Charles, David A. (pseud.). "The Dismissal of Marshal P'eng Teh-huai," *China Quarterly*, 8 (Oct.–Dec. 1961).

Chen, C. S., ed. *Rural People's Communes in Lien-chiang ... 1962–1963.* Stanford, Calif.: Hoover Institution, 1969.

China's Legal and Security Systems. London, 1969.

Chornovil, Vyacheslav. *The Chornovil Papers.* New York: McGraw-Hill, 1969.

Chukovskaya, Lydia. *The Deserted House.* New York: Dutton, 1967.

Cohen, Arthur A. *The Communism of Mao Tse-tung.* Chicago: University of Chicago Press, 1964.

Cohen, Jerome. "The Criminal Process in China," in Treadgold, listed below.

Commission Internationale Contre le Régime Concentrationnaire. *White Book on Forced Labour and Concentration Camps in the People's Republic of China.* 2 vols. Paris, 1957–58.

Communist China 1955–1959: Policy Documents with Analysis. Cambridge, Mass.: Harvard University Press, 1962.

Conquest, Robert. *The Great Terror.* New York: Macmillan, 1968.

———. *Power and Policy in the USSR.* New York: St. Martin's, 1961.

———. *The Soviet Deportation of Nationalities.* New York: Praeger, 1960.

Coser, Lewis. *The Functions of Social Conflict.* New York: Free Press, 1956.

Cyert, Richard M., and James G. March. *A Behavioral Theory of the Firm.* Englewood Cliffs, N.J.: Prentice-Hall, 1963.

Dahl, Robert A., ed. *Political Oppositions in Western Democracies*. New Haven, Conn.: Yale University Press, 1966.

Dahrendorf, Ralf. *Class and Class Conflict in Industrial Society*. Stanford, Calif.: Stanford University Press, 1959.

————. *Essays in the Theory of Society*. Stanford, Calif.: Stanford University Press, 1968.

Dallin, Alexander, et al., eds. *Diversity in International Communism*. New York: Columbia University Press, 1963.

Dallin, Alexander, and Thomas B. Larson, eds. *Soviet Politics Since Khrushchev*. Englewood Cliffs, N.J.: Prentice-Hall, 1968.

Dallin, David J., and Boris Nicolaevsky. *Forced Labor in Soviet Russia*. New Haven, Conn.: Yale University Press, 1948.

Dedijer, Vladimir. *Tito*. New York: Simon and Schuster, 1953.

Dellin, Lubomir. "Agriculture and the Peasant," in Fisher-Galati, listed below.

Demerath, Nicholas J., and Richard A. Peterson, eds. *System, Change, and Conflict*. New York: Free Press, 1967.

Deutsch, Karl W. "Cracks in the Monolith," in Friedrich, ed., *Totalitarianism*, listed below.

Devlin, Kevin. "The Permanent Revolution of Fidel Castro," *Problems of Communism*, XVII, 1 (Jan.–Feb. 1968).

Dewar, Hugo. *The Modern Inquisition*. London: Wingate, 1953.

Dewey, John. "Force and Coercion," *International Journal of Ethics*, XXVI (1915–16).

D'iakov, Boris. *Povest' o perezhitom*. Moscow: Sovetskaia Rossiia, 1966.

Dostoyevsky, Fyodor. *The Possessed*. New York: Macmillan, 1931.

Draper, Theodore. *Castroism, Theory and Practice*. New York: Praeger, 1965.

Dzyuba, Ivan. *Internationalism or Russification?* London: Weidenfeld, 1968.

Eckstein, Harry, ed. *Internal War*. New York: Free Press, 1964.

Ehrenburg, Ilya. *Memoirs, 1921–1941*. New York: World, 1963.

Ellison, Herbert. "The Decision to Collectivize Agriculture," *American Slavic and East European Review*, XX, 2 (April 1961).

Emmet, Dorothy. *Function, Purpose, and Powers*. London: Macmillan, 1958.

Entsiklopedia gosudarstva i prava. 3 vols. Moscow: Kommunisticheskaia Akademiia, 1927.

Eropkin, Mikhail. *Upravlenie v oblasti okhrany obshchestvennogo poriadka.* Moscow: Iur. Lit., 1965.

Etzioni, Amitai. *The Active Society.* New York: Free Press, 1968.

——. *A Comparative Analysis of Complex Organizations.* New York: Free Press, 1961.

——, ed. *Complex Organizations: A Sociological Reader.* New York: Holt, Rinehart and Winston, 1961.

——, ed. *A Sociological Reader on Complex Organizations,* 2d ed. New York: Holt, Rinehart and Winston, 1969.

Fainsod, Merle. "Bureaucracy and Modernization: The Russian and Soviet Case," in LaPalombara, listed below.

——. *How Russia Is Ruled.* Cambridge, Mass.: Harvard University Press, 1953. Rev. ed. 1964.

——. *Smolensk Under Soviet Rule.* Cambridge, Mass.: Harvard University Press, 1958.

——. "Transformations in the Communist Party of the Soviet Union," in Treadgold, listed below.

Feifer, George. *Justice in Moscow.* New York: Simon and Schuster, 1964.

Feiwel, George. *The Soviet Quest for Economic Efficiency.* New York: Praeger, 1967.

Festinger, Leon. *A Theory of Cognitive Dissonance.* Stanford, Calif.: Stanford University Press, 1962.

Fisher-Galati, Stephen, ed. *Eastern Europe in the Sixties.* New York: Praeger, 1963.

Fleron, Frederic J. "Toward a Reconceptualization of Political Change in the Soviet Union," *Comparative Politics,* I, 2 (Jan. 1969).

Frame, William V. "Dialectical Historicism and the Terror in Chinese Communism," unpub. diss., University of Washington, 1969.

Friedrich, Carl J., ed. *Totalitarianism.* Cambridge, Mass.: Harvard University Press, 1954.

——. "Totalitarianism: Recent Trends," *Problems of Communism,* XVII, 3 (May–June 1968).

Friedrich, Carl J., and Zbigniew Brzezinski. *Totalitarian Dictatorship and Autocracy,* rev. ed. by Friedrich. Cambridge, Mass.: Harvard University Press, 1965.

Friedrich, Carl J., et al. *Totalitarianism in Perspective.* New York: Praeger, 1969.

Fryer, Peter. *Hungarian Tragedy.* London: Dennis Dobson, 1956.

Gamarnikow, Michael. *Economic Reforms in Eastern Europe.* Detroit: Wayne State University Press, 1968.

Gaucher, Roland. *Opposition in the USSR, 1917–1967.* New York: Funk and Wagnalls, 1969.

Geertz, Clifford, ed. *Old Societies and New States.* New York: Free Press, 1963.

Gerschenkron, Alexander. *Continuity in History.* Cambridge, Mass.: Harvard University Press, 1968.

Gerth, H. H., and C. Wright Mills, eds. *From Max Weber: Essays in Sociology.* New York: Oxford University Press, 1958.

Ginzburg, Alexander, ed. *Belaia Kniga po delu A. Siniavskogo i Yu. Danielia.* Frankfurt: Posev, 1967.

Ginzburg, Eugenia. *Journey into the Whirlwind.* New York: Harcourt, Brace, 1967.

Gittings, John. *The Role of the Chinese Army.* London: Oxford University Press, 1967.

Gliksman, Jerzy. "Social Prophylaxis as a Form of Soviet Terror," in Friedrich, ed., *Totalitarianism,* listed above.

Goffman, Erving. *Asylums.* Garden City, N.Y.: Doubleday, 1961.

Gorbatov, Alexander. *Years Off My Life.* New York: W. W. Norton, 1965.

Greenstein, Fred I. *Personality and Politics.* Chicago: Markham, 1969.

Gregor, A. James. "Political Science and the Uses of Functional Analysis," *American Political Science Review,* LXII, 2 (June 1968).

Griffith, William E., ed. *Albania and the Sino-Soviet Rift.* Cambridge, Mass.: MIT Press, 1963.

———, ed. *European Communism,* vol. I. Cambridge, Mass.: MIT Press, 1964.

Gross, Feliks. *The Seizure of Political Power.* New York: Philosophical Library, 1958.

Gross, Llewellyn, ed. *Symposium on Sociological Theory.* New York: Harper and Row, 1959.

Gundersheim, Arthur. "Terror and Political Control in Communist China," unpub. paper. Center for Social Organization Studies, University of Chicago, 1966.

Halperin, Ernst. *The Triumphant Heretic.* London: Heinemann, 1958.

Hammer, Darrell. "Law Enforcement, Social Control and the Withering of the State," *Soviet Studies,* XIV, 4 (Apr. 1963).

Hayward, Max, and Leopold Labedz, eds. *Literature and Revolution in the Soviet Union.* London: Oxford University Press, 1963.

———. *On Trial: The Case of Sinyavsky (Tertz) and Daniel (Arzhak).* London: Collins and Harvell, 1967.

Hazard, John N. *Communists and their Law.* Chicago: University of Chicago Press, 1969.

———. *Law and Social Change in the USSR.* London: Stevens, 1953.

Hempel, Carl G. "The Logic of Functional Analysis," in Llewellyn Gross, listed above.

Hinkle, Lawrence. "Health, Human Ecology, and the Hungarian Revolution," unpub. paper. New York: Society for the Study of Human Ecology, 1958.

Ho, Ping-ti, and Tang Tsou, eds. *China in Crisis.* 3 vols. Chicago: University of Chicago Press, 1968.

Hoffman, George, and Fred W. Neal. *Yugoslavia.* New York: Twentieth Century Fund, 1962.

Hoffmann, Charles. *Work Incentive Practices and Policies in the People's Republic of China, 1953–1965.* Albany: State University of New York Press, 1967.

Hollander, Paul J. "Models of Behavior in Stalinist Literature," *American Sociological Review,* XXXI, 3 (June 1966).

———. "The New Man and His Enemies: A Study of the Stalinist Conceptions of Good and Evil Personified," unpub. diss., Princeton University, 1963. Abstract in University Microfilms 64-6271.

Ignotus, Paul. "The AVH: Symbol of Terror," *Problems of Communism,* VI, 5 (Sept. 1957).

———. *Political Prisoner.* New York: Collier, 1964.

Inkeles, Alex. "The Totalitarian Mystique," in Friedrich, ed., *Totalitarianism,* listed above.

Inkeles, Alex, and Raymond A. Bauer. *The Soviet Citizen.* Cambridge, Mass.: Harvard University Press, 1959.

Insko, C. A., et al. "Effects of High and Low Fear-Arousing Communication upon Opinion . . . ," *Journal of Experimental Social Psychology,* I (1965).

Institute for the Study of the USSR. *Genocide in the USSR.* New York: Scarecrow Press, 1958.

Inter-American Commission on Human Rights. *Report on the Situation of Political Prisoners and Their Relatives in Cuba.* Washington, D.C.: Pan-American Union, 1963.

International Encyclopedia of the Social Sciences. New York: Macmillan, 1968.

Ionescu, Ghiţa. *Communism in Rumania*. London: Oxford University Press, 1965.

―――. *The Politics of the European Communist States*. New York: Praeger, 1968.

Iz istorii Vserossiiskoi Chrezvychainoi Komissii 1917–1921 gg.; sbornik dokumentov. Moscow, Gospolitizdat., 1958.

Janis, Irving. "Effects of Fear Arousal on Attitude Change," in Berkowitz, listed above.

Janos, Andrew C. "The Communist Theory of the State and Revolution," in Black and Thornton, listed above.

Jasny, Naum. "Labor and Output in Soviet Concentration Camps," *Journal of Political Economy*, LIX, 5 (Oct. 1951).

Johnson, Chalmers A. "Building a Communist Nation in China," in Scalapino, listed below.

―――, ed. *Change in Communist Systems*. Stanford, Calif.: Stanford University Press, 1970.

―――. "Chinese Communist Leadership and Mass Response: The Yenan Period and the Socialist Education Campaign Period," in Ho and Tsou, I, listed above.

―――. *Peasant Nationalism and Communist Power*. Stanford, Calif.: Stanford University Press, 1962.

―――. *Revolutionary Change*. Boston: Little, Brown, 1966.

Johnson, Priscilla. *Khrushchev and the Arts: The Politics of Soviet Culture*. Cambridge, Mass.: MIT Press, 1965.

Jowitt, Kenneth T. "A Comparative Analysis of Leninist and Nationalist Elite Ideologies and Nation-Building Strategies," unpub. paper. Berkeley: University of California, 1968.

Kamenka, Eugene. "The Soviet View of Law," *Problems of Communism*, XIV, 2 (Mar.–Apr. 1965).

Kaplan, Karel. "Zamyšlení nad politickými procesy," *Nová Mysl* (Prague), 6–8 (1968).

―――. *Život Strany*, 29 (Nov. 27, 1968).

Karcz, Jerzy, ed. *Soviet and East European Agriculture*. Berkeley: University of California Press, 1967.

Kardelj, Edvard. *Problemi socijalističke politike na selu*. Belgrade: Kultura, 1959.

Kecskemeti, Paul. *The Unexpected Revolution*. Stanford, Calif.: Stanford University Press, 1961.

Kirchheimer, Otto. "Confining Conditions and Revolutionary Breakthroughs," *American Political Science Review,* LIX, 4 (Dec. 1965).

———. *Political Justice.* Princeton, N.J.: Princeton University Press, 1961.

Koestler, Arthur. *Darkness at Noon.* New York: Signet, 1948.

Korbonski, Andrzej. "The Agricultural Problem in East Central Europe," *Journal of International Affairs,* XX, 1 (1966).

———. "Peasant Agriculture in Socialist Poland Since 1956: An Alternative to Collectivization," in Karcz, listed above.

———. *Politics of Socialist Agriculture in Poland 1945–1960.* New York: Columbia University Press, 1965.

Kornhauser, William. *The Politics of Mass Society.* Glencoe, Ill.: Free Press, 1959.

Kraus, Wolfgang H., and Gabriel A. Almond. "Resistance and Repression Under the Nazis," in Almond, *The Struggle for Democracy,* listed above.

Kronrod, Ya. "Ekonomicheskaia reforma i nekotorye problemy politicheskoi ekonomii sotsializma," *Voprosy ekonomiki,* 10, 1966.

LaPalombara, Joseph, ed. *Bureaucracy and Political Development.* Princeton, N.J.: Princeton University Press, 1965.

Lapenna, Ivo. *Soviet Penal Policy.* London: Bodley Head, 1968.

LaPiere, Richard T. *A Theory of Social Control.* New York: McGraw-Hill, 1954.

Lasswell, Harold. *Psychopathology and Politics,* rev. ed. New York: Viking, 1960.

Latsis, Martin (pseud.). *Chrezvychainye Komissii.* Moscow, Gosizdat, 1921.

———. *Dva goda bor'by na vnutrennem fronte.* Moscow, Gosizdat, 1920.

Lazarus, Richard S. *Psychological Stress and the Coping Process.* New York: McGraw-Hill, 1966.

Lazarus, Richard S., et al. "The Effects of Psychological Stress upon Performance," *Psychological Bulletin,* XLIX, 4 (1952).

Lazitch, Branko. "Le martyrologie du Comintern," *Le Contrat Social,* IX, 6 (Nov.–Dec. 1965).

Lenin, Vladimir. *Polnoe sobranie sochinenii,* 5th ed. Moscow: Politizdat, 1958–65.

Leonhard, Wolfgang. *The Kremlin After Stalin.* New York: Praeger, 1962.

———. "Politics and Ideology in the Post-Khrushchev Era," in Dallin and Larson, listed above.

Leventhal, N., et al. "The Effects of Fear . . . upon Attitudes and Behavior," *Journal of Personal and Social Psychology*, II (1965).

LeVine, Robert. "Political Socialization and Culture Change," in Geertz, listed above.

Levitt, Eugene E. *The Psychology of Anxiety*. Indianapolis, Ind.: Bobbs-Merrill, 1967.

Lewin, Moshe. "The Immediate Background of Soviet Collectivization," *Soviet Studies*, XVII, 2 (Oct. 1956).

———. *Russian Peasants and Soviet Power*. London: Allen and Unwin, 1968.

Lewis, Flora. *Red Pawn: The Story of Noel Field*. Garden City, N.Y.: Doubleday, 1965.

Lewis, John W. "China's Secret Military Papers," *China Quarterly*, 18 (Apr.–June 1964).

———. "Social Limits of Politically Induced Change," in Morse et al., listed below.

Lewytzkyj, Borys. *Die rote Inquisition*. Frankfurt: Societäts-Verlag, 1967.

———. *Vom roten Terror zur sozialistischen Gesetzlichkeit*. Munich: Nymphenburger Verlag, 1961.

Lieberthal, Kenneth. "Tactics, Goals and Social Composition: Differences Between the Soviet and Chinese Communist Parties," unpub. paper. New York: Columbia University, 1969.

Lifton, Robert Jay. *Revolutionary Immortality: Mao Tse-tung and the Chinese Cultural Revolution*. New York: Random House, 1968.

———. *Thought Reform and the Psychology of Totalism*. New York: W. W. Norton, 1961.

Lipset, Seymour Martin. *Political Man*. Garden City, N.Y.: Doubleday, 1960.

Lipson, Leon. "Law: The Function of Extra-Judicial Mechanisms," in Treadgold, listed below.

———. "The New Face of Socialist Legality," *Problems of Communism*, VII, 4 (July–Aug. 1958); "Socialist Legality," *ibid.*, VIII, 2 (Mar.–Apr. 1959); "Hosts and Pests," *ibid.*, XIV, 2 (Mar.–Apr. 1965).

Lithuanian Bulletin. New York, 1945–49.

Litvinov, Pavel. *The Demonstration in Pushkin Square*. Boston: Gambit, 1969.

Loebl, Eugen. *Stalinism in Prague*. New York: Grove, 1969.

London, Artur. *L'aveu*. Paris: Gallimard, 1969.

London, Kurt, ed. *The Soviet Union: A Half-Century of Communism*. Baltimore, Md.: Johns Hopkins Press, 1968.

Lowenthal, Leo. "Terror's Atomization of Man," *Commentary*, I (Jan. 1946).

Lowenthal, Richard. "Soviet and Chinese World Views," in Treadgold, listed below.

———. *World Communism*. New York: Oxford University Press, 1964.

MacFarquhar, Roderick. *The Hundred Flowers Campaign and the Chinese Intellectuals*. New York: Praeger, 1960.

Madge, John. "Attitudes of Refugee Respondents," unpub. paper. New York: Columbia University Research Project on Hungary, 1958.

Marchenko, Anatoli. *My Testimony*. New York: Dutton, 1969.

Marcuse, Herbert. *Soviet Marxism*. New York: Columbia University Press, 1958.

Marko, Kurt. *Evolution wider Willen*. Graz: Böhlaus, 1968.

Marx, Karl, and Friedrich Engels. *Werke (Institut für Marxismus-Leninismus beim ZK der SED)*, XXXIII. Berlin: Dietz, 1966.

Massachusetts Institute of Technology, Center for International Studies. "The Takeover of Eastern Europe," unpub. series of papers.

Maulnier, Thierry. *La face de Méduse du communisme*. Paris: Gallimard, 1951.

May, Rollo. "Centrality of the Problem of Anxiety in Our Day," in Stein et al., listed below.

McCallum, Douglas. "Obstacles to Change in a Communist System," in Miller and Rigby, listed below.

McCleery, Richard H. "Policy Change in Prison Management," in Etzioni, *Complex Organizations*, listed above.

McVicker, Charles P. *Titoism*. New York: St. Martin's Press, 1957.

Medalie, Richard J. "The Policy of Takeover: The Stages of Totalitarian Development in Eastern Europe," *Public Policy*, VII (1956).

Medvedev, Zhores. *The Rise and Fall of T. D. Lysenko*. New York: Columbia University Press, 1969.

Meissner, Boris. "Totalitarian Rule and Social Change in the Soviet Union," *Modern World* (Dusseldorf), V (1967).

Mel'gunov, Sergei. *The Red Terror in Russia.* London: Dent, 1925.

Merleau-Ponty, Maurice. *Humanism and Terror.* Boston: Beacon, 1969.

Merton, Robert K. *On Theoretical Sociology.* New York: Free Press, 1967.

————. *Social Theory and Social Structure,* enl. ed. New York: Free Press, 1968.

Meyer, Alfred G. *The Soviet Political System.* New York: Random House, 1965.

————. "USSR, Incorporated," *Slavic Review,* XX, 3 (Oct. 1961).

Miliutin, V. P., et al. "Zaiavlenie gruppy narodnykh komissarov," in Institut Marksizma-Leninizma pri TsK KPSS, *Protokoly Tsentral'nogo Komiteta RSDRP(b): avgust 1917–fevral' 1918.* Moscow: IML, 1958.

Miller, J. D. B., and T. H. Rigby, eds. *The Disintegrating Monolith.* Canberra: Australian National University, 1965.

Miller, J. G. "Toward a General Theory for the Behavioral Sciences," *American Psychologist,* 10 (1955).

Mills, Harriet C. "Thought Reform: Ideological Remolding in China," *Atlantic Monthly,* 204 (Dec. 1959).

Mironov, N. "O sochetanii ubezhdeniia i prinuzhdeniia," *Kommunist* (Moscow), 3 (1961).

Mitrany, David. *Marx Against the Peasant,* rev. ed. New York: Crowell-Collier, 1961.

Moore, Barrington. *Political Power and Social Theory.* Cambridge, Mass.: Harvard University Press, 1958.

————. *Soviet Politics: The Dilemma of Power,* rev. ed. New York: Harper, 1965.

————. *Terror and Progress—USSR.* Cambridge, Mass.: Harvard University Press, 1954.

Morse, Chandler, et al. *Modernization by Design.* Ithaca, N.Y.: Cornell University Press, 1969.

Nagel, Ernest. *The Structure of Science.* New York: Harcourt, Brace, 1961.

Nagy, Imre. *On Communism.* New York: Praeger, 1957.

Narkiewicz, Olga A. "Stalin, War Communism and Collectivization," *Soviet Studies,* XVIII, 1 (July 1966).

Neubauer, Deane A., and Lawrence D. Kastner. "The Study of Compliance Maintenance as a Strategy for Comparative Research," *World Politics*, XXI, 4 (July 1969).

Neuhauser, Charles. "The Chinese Communist Party in the 1960's: Prelude to the Cultural Revolution," *China Quarterly*, 32 (Oct.– Dec. 1967).

Neumann, Franz. *The Democratic and the Authoritarian State*. New York: Free Press, 1957.

Neumann, Sigmund. *Permanent Revolution*, 2d ed. New York: Praeger, 1965.

Nicolaevsky, Boris. *Power and the Soviet Elite*. New York: Praeger, 1965.

Nove, Alec. *Economic Rationality and Soviet Politics*. New York: Praeger, 1964.

"Observer" (pseud.). *Message from Moscow*. New York: Knopf, 1969.

O'Connor, Dennis. "Soviet People's Guards: An Experiment with Civil Police," *New York University Law Review*, XXXIX, 4 (June 1964).

Oksenberg, Michel. "Local Leaders in Rural China, 1962–1965," in Barnett, *Chinese Communist Politics*, listed above.

———. "Policy Formulation in Communist China: The Case of the Mass Irrigation Campaign, 1957–58," unpub. diss., Columbia University, 1969.

Oren, Mordekhai. *Prisonnier politique à Prague*. Paris: Juilliard, 1960.

Orlov, Alexander. *The Secret History of Stalin's Crimes*. New York: Random House, 1953.

Pasternak, Boris. *Doctor Zhivago*. New York: Pantheon, 1958.

Peterson, Joseph. *The Great Leap—China*. Bombay: B. I. Publications, 1966.

Petrov, Vladimir, trans. and ed. *June Twenty-Second, Nineteen Forty-One*. Columbia: University of South Carolina Press, 1968.

Poretsky, Elizabeth. *Our Own People*. London: Oxford University Press, 1969.

Pye, Lucian. *The Spirit of Chinese Politics*. Cambridge, Mass.: MIT Press, 1968.

Reve, Karel van het, comp. *Dear Comrade*. New York: Pitman, 1969.

Richert, Ernst. *Macht ohne Mandat*. Cologne: Westdeutscher Verlag, 1963.

Rickett, Allyn, and Adele Rickett. *Prisoners of the Liberation*. New York: Cameron Associates, 1957.

Rigby, T. Harry. *Communist Party Membership in the USSR*. Princeton, N.J.: Princeton University Press, 1968.

Ritvo, Herbert. "Totalitarianism Without Coercion?" *Problems of Communism*, IX, 6 (Nov.–Dec. 1960).

Romashkin, P. S. "O roli ubezhdeniia i prinuzhdeniia v Sovetskom gosudarstve," *Sovetskoe gosudarstvo i pravo*, 2 (1960).

Roucek, Joseph S. "Sociological Elements of a Theory of Terror and Violence," *American Journal of Economics and Sociology*, XXI, 2 (1962).

Russell, Bertrand. *Power*. London: Allen and Unwin, 1938.

Sabatini, Rafael. *Torquemada and the Spanish Inquisition*. Boston: Houghton Mifflin, 1924.

Sakharov, Andrei. *Progress, Coexistence and Intellectual Freedom*. New York: W. W. Norton, 1968.

Sanders, Irwin T., ed. *Collectivization of Agriculture in Eastern Europe*. Lexington: University of Kentucky Press, 1958.

Savarius, Vincent (pseud.). *Freiwillige für den Galgen*. Cologne: Wissenschaft und Politik, 1963.

Scalapino, Robert A., ed. *The Communist Revolution in Asia*. Englewood Cliffs, N.J.: Prentice-Hall, 1965.

Schapiro, Leonard. "Collective Lack of Leadership," *Survey*, 70–71 (Winter–Spring 1969).

———. *The Communist Party of the Soviet Union*. New York: Random House, 1959.

———. *The Origin of the Communist Autocracy*. Cambridge, Mass.: Harvard University Press, 1955.

Scharndorff, Werner. *Moskaus permanente Säuberung*. Munich: Olzog, 1964.

Schein, Edgar, et al. *Coercive Persuasion*. New York: W. W. Norton, 1961.

Schram, Stuart. *Mao Tse-tung*. New York: Simon and Schuster, 1962.

Schurmann, Franz. *Ideology and Organization in Communist China*, 2d ed. Berkeley: University of California Press, 1968.

———. "Organization and Response in Communist China," *The Annals of the Academy of Political and Social Science*, 321 (Jan. 1959).

Schwartz, Solomon. *Evrei v Sovetskom Soiuze ... 1939–1965 gg*. New York: American Jewish Labor Committee, 1966.

Seeman, Melvin. "On the Meaning of Alienation," *American Sociological Review*, XXIV, 6 (Dec. 1959).

Selye, Hans. *The Stress of Life*. New York: McGraw-Hill, 1956.

Selznick, Philip. *The Organizational Weapon*. New York: McGraw-Hill, 1951.

Seton-Watson, Hugh. *The East European Revolution*. London: Methuen, 1952.

Shitarev, G. "Partiia i stroitel'stvo kommunizma," *Politicheskoe samoobrazovanie*, 8 (1960).

Simmonds, J. D. "P'eng Te-huai: A Chronological Reexamination," *China Quarterly*, 37 (Jan.–Mar. 1969).

Skilling, H. Gordon. "Background to the Study of Opposition in Communist Eastern Europe," *Government and Opposition*, III, 3 (1968).

Skilling, H. Gordon, and Franklyn Griffiths, eds. *Interest Groups in Soviet Politics*. Princeton, N.J.: Princeton University Press, forthcoming.

Skinner, G. William, and Edwin A. Winckler. "Compliance Succession in Rural Communist China: A Cyclical Theory," in Etzioni, *Sociological Reader*, listed above.

Slánský, Josefa. *Report on My Husband*. London: Hutchinson, 1969.

Slusser, Robert M., and Simon Wolin, eds. *The Soviet Secret Police*. New York: Praeger, 1957.

Sofinov, Pavel G. *Ocherki istorii VChK (1917–1922 gg.)*. Moscow: Gospolitizdat., 1960.

Solzhenitsyn, Alexander. *The Cancer Ward*. New York: Bantam, 1969.

———. *The First Circle*. New York: Harper, 1968.

Stein, Maurice, et al. *Identity and Anxiety*. Glencoe, Ill., Free Press, 1960.

Steinberg, I. N. *Gewalt und Terror in der Revolution*. Berlin: Rowohlt, 1931.

———. *In the Workshop of the Revolution*. New York: Rinehart, 1953.

Suárez, Andrés. *Cuba: Castroism and Communism, 1959–1966*. Cambridge, Mass.: MIT Press, 1967.

Swianiewicz, S. *Forced Labour and Economic Development*. London: Oxford University Press, 1965.

Swiatlo, Józef. *Behind the Scene of the Party and Bezpieka*. New York: Radio Free Europe, 1955.

Szamuely, Tibor. "The Elimination of Opposition Between the 16th and 17th Congresses of the CPSU," *Soviet Studies*, XVII, 3 (Jan. 1966).

Tatu, Michel. "In Quest of Justice," *Problems of Communism,* XII, 4–5 (July–Oct. 1968).

———. *Power in the Kremlin.* New York: Viking, 1969.

Thornton, Thomas P. "Terror as a Weapon of Political Agitation," in Eckstein, listed above.

Treadgold, Donald W., ed. *Soviet and Chinese Communism.* Seattle: University of Washington Press, 1967.

Trotsky, Lev. *Lenin.* New York: Capricorn, 1962.

———. *Terrorism and Communism.* Ann Arbor: University of Michigan Press, 1961.

Tsou, Tang. "Revolution, Reintegration, and Crisis in Communist China," in Ho and Tsou, I, listed above.

Tucker, Robert C. "The Deradicalization of Marxist Movements," *American Political Science Review,* LXI, 2 (June 1967).

———. "Paths of Communist Revolution, 1917–1967," in Kurt London, listed above.

Tucker, Robert C., and Stephen F. Cohen, eds. *The Great Purge Trial.* New York: Universal Library, 1965.

Ulč, Otto. "Koestler Revisited," *Survey,* 72 (Summer 1969).

Unger, A. L. "Stalin's Renewal of the Leading Stratum: A Note on the Great Purge," *Soviet Studies,* XX, 3 (Jan. 1969).

Valentinov, Nikolai. *Encounters with Lenin.* London: Oxford University Press, 1968.

Vogel, Ezra. "From Friendship to Comradeship: The Change in Personal Relations in Communist China," *China Quarterly,* 21 (Jan.–Mar. 1965).

———. "Land Reform in Kwangtung, 1951–1953," *China Quarterly,* 39 (July–Sept. 1969).

———. "Voluntarism and Social Control," in Treadgold, listed above.

Vserossiiskaia Chrezvychainaia Komissiia. Krasnaia Kniga, Vol. I. Moscow: VCheKa, 1920.

Wagner, Helmut. "Die Rolle des Terrors und des Persönlichkeitskultes in der Sowjetunion," *Osteuropa,* 10–11 (1967).

Wallach, Erica. *Light at Midnight.* Garden City, N.Y.: Doubleday, 1967.

Walter, Eugene V. "Power and Violence," *American Political Science Review,* LVIII, 2 (June 1964).

———. *Terror and Resistance.* New York: Oxford University Press, 1969.

Weissberg, Alexander. *The Accused.* New York: Simon and Schuster, 1951.

Werth, Alexander. *Russia, Hopes and Fears.* New York: Simon and Schuster, 1969.

Whitaker, Carl A., and Thomas Malone. "Anxiety and Psychotherapy," in Stein et al., listed above.

Wilber, Charles K. *The Soviet Model and Underdeveloped Countries.* Chapel Hill: University of North Carolina Press, 1969.

Withey, Stephen B. "Reaction to Uncertain Threat," in Baker and Chapman, listed above.

Wolin, Sheldon S. "Violence and the Western Political Tradition," *American Journal of Orthopsychiatry,* XXXIII: 1 (Jan. 1963).

Yakir, Piotr. Letter to editor of *Kommunist* (Moscow), trans. in *Problems of Communism,* XVIII, 4–5 (July–Oct. 1969).

Yang, C. K. *A Chinese Village in Early Communist Transition.* Cambridge, Mass.: Harvard University Press, 1959.

Yu, Frederick T. C. *Mass Persuasion in China.* New York: Praeger, 1964.

Zinner, Paul. *Communist Strategy and Tactics in Czechoslovakia.* New York: Praeger, 1963.

———. *Revolution in Hungary.* New York: Columbia University Press, 1962.

Zolotukhin, G. S. "Stavka na doverie," *Oktiabr',* 10 (1965).

Index

Index

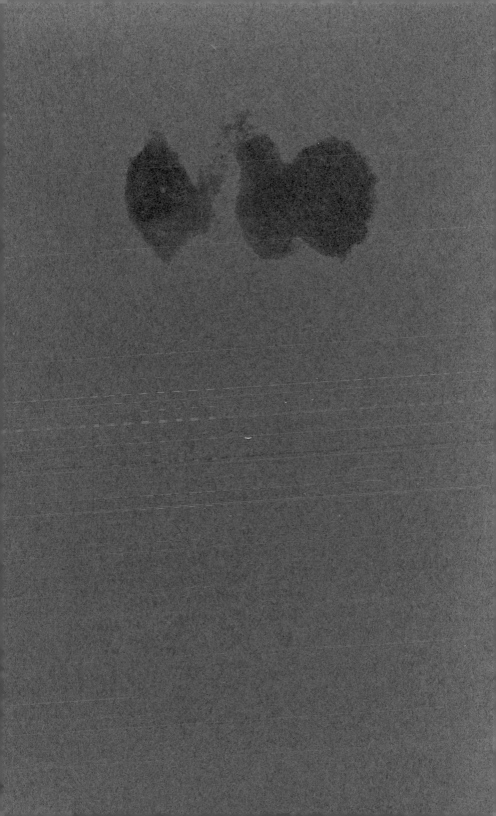

DUE

75